All About Chords

■

E L V O   S .   D ' A M A N T E

All About Chords

A comprehensive approach to understanding contemporary chordal structures and progressions through solid drills in suggested study questions, keyboard drills, and ear-training exercises.

Elvo S. D' Amante
Chairman, Department of Music
Laney Community College

ENCORE MUSIC PUBLISHING COMPANY

Library of Congress Cataloging-in-Publication Data

D'Amante, Elvo S. (date)
    All about chords.

    Includes index.
    1. Harmony.   I. Title.
MT50.D123   1988   781'.22   88-24571

ISBN   0-9620941-0-2

Copyright 1988 Encore Music Publishing Company
          P.O. Box 315   Orinda, CA 94563

10 9 8 7 6 5 4 3 2 1

To all of my students

past, present, and future

C O N T E N T S

P A R T I

[Triads]

P A R T II

[Seventh Chords]

P A R T III

P A R T IV

□

□

x

PART V

[Addendum]

Acknowledgments

Thoughts and ideas found within the pages of a textbook are never a totally singular, individual endeavor; but, rather, a combination of formal training, empirical knowledge and a distillation of personal interactions with one's past teachers, professional associates, and friends, a setting in which encouragement, direction, and motivation play positive and productive roles. Former students, colleagues, and professional acquaintances have all contributed to this project in one way or another. Without their much valued support, none of this would have taken place.

I owe special thanks to two of my colleagues at Laney, Messrs. Tom Hibdon and Ed Kelly; their support has always been forthcoming and truly a source of inspiration. Also, I owe much of what I've accomplished in my teaching and professional careers to the inspiration and encouragement of two of my most honored master teachers, Messrs. Darius Milhaud and Roger Sessions, without whom none of this would have been possible.

Finally, I wish to thank all of my former students who unwittingly planted the seed for this textbook and to all my present students who daily motivate and guide me in my constant search for excellence in teaching.

The Inventory Mini-Exam: Key Signatures and Intervals

TO THE STUDENT:

The following mini-exam is to be looked upon as an inventory examination. It is important that you take this test before doing the text materials. If you should score below **sixty percent (60%)** on this examination and wish to improve your preparedness for the forthcoming materials, you should purchase a copy of <u>Music Fundamentals</u> by the author of this text at your local music or college book store and place special emphasis on studying Chapters Five, Seven, and Eight. Be sure to do all of the drills at the end of each chapter. A thorough study of <u>major</u> and <u>minor</u> <u>key signatures</u> and <u>intervals</u> will sufficiently prepare you for the successful completion of all of the materials in this text.

<u>Directions for scoring your exam:</u>

Each answer must be entirely correct. For example, if one sharp is misplaced in a key signature, the entire key signature is incorrect. Also, if an enharmonic pitch is used instead of the exact pitch, the interval must be counted as incorrect. **Sixty percent (60%)** or **above** would be a <u>passing grade</u> on this examination.

Tally up your <u>correct</u> responses and multiply your total by <u>two</u> in order to arrive at the <u>total</u> <u>percentage</u> <u>correct</u>.

For example:

Question	#1	6	correct	out of	8	possible	points
"	#2	7	"	" "	7	"	"
"	#3	13	"	" "	15	"	"
"	#4	14	"	" "	15	"	"
"	#5	5	"	" "	5	"	"
		45			50		

$$45 \times 2 = 90\%$$

thus: **Forty-five (45)** <u>correct</u> responses out of **fifty (50%)** possible points times <u>two</u> equals **ninety percent (90%)** for a good passing grade!

The **Inventory Mini-Exam** is located on the next two pages; the correct answers are supplied on <u>page</u> <u>115</u> of the **Addendum**.

Possible
Points:

[8]   1. <u>Identify</u> the following **major** key signatures.

[7]   2. While providing your best manuscript, <u>supply</u> the following **major** key signatures.

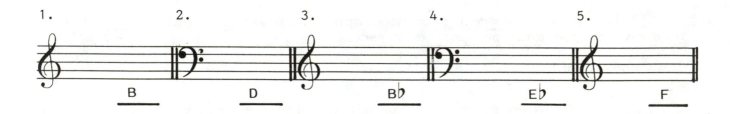

[15] 3. Identify the following harmonic intervals.

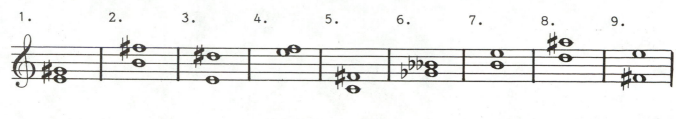

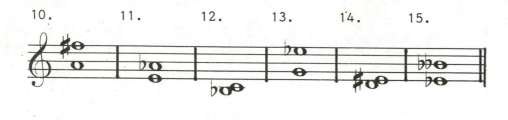

[15] 4. Supply the missing upper pitch to complete the desired harmonic
     interval. Use double sharps and double flats whenever necessary.

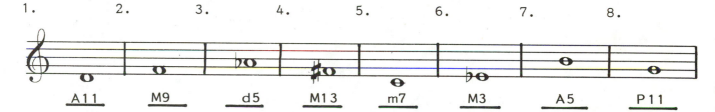

A11   M9   d5   M13   m7   M3   A5   P11

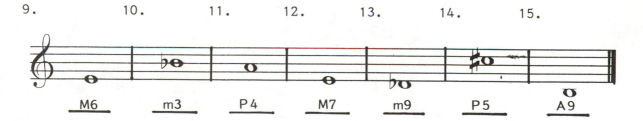

M6   m3   P4   M7   m9   P5   A9

[5] 5. Supply the missing lower pitch to complete the desired harmonic
    interval. Use double sharps and double flats whenever necessary.

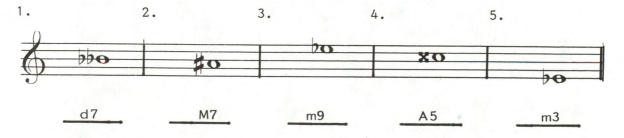

d7   M7   m9   A5   m3

P A R T   I

TRIADS

Triads are constructed in the following manner: they all contain a **root** tone, which represents the letter name of the chord; a **third**, which represents the interval of a third above the root tone; and a **fifth**, which represents the interval of a fifth above the root tone.

Example No. 1

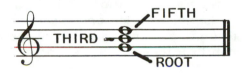

For the purposes of this study there are <u>four basic triads</u> and <u>two variations</u> for a total of **six** triadic categories:

[1]   the <u>Major Triad</u>;

[2]   the <u>Minor Triad</u>;

[3]   the <u>Augmented Triad</u>;

[4]   the <u>Diminished Triad</u>; plus the two variations

[5]   the <u>Major Triad With The Lowered Fifth</u>; and

[6]   the <u>Suspended Triad</u>.

[1] THE MAJOR TRIAD

As was previously shown, a triad contains three tones: a **root** tone; a **third**; and a **fifth**. The quality of the triad is **major** when the distance between its **root** and its **third** is **major** and its **fifth** -- that distance between the **root** and the **fifth** -- is **perfect**. Or, in other words, a **major triad** consists of **two** successive intervals of a **third**, the first interval representing the distance of a **major third** and the second interval representing the distance of a **minor third**.

1

Example No. 2

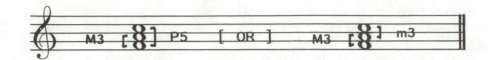

In the Alphabetical Chord System use only the capital letter representing the **root tone** and **accidental**, if needed, to designate a **major triad.** No modifying words, abbreviations, or symbols such as major, maj., ma., Δ, etc., are ever used to symbolize a **major triad.**

Example No. 3

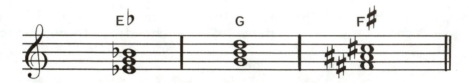

[2] THE MINOR TRIAD

The **minor triad** contains a **minor** third and a **perfect** fifth above the root. Or, in other words, a **minor triad** consists of two successive intervals of a third, the first interval representing the distance of a **minor third** and the second interval representing the distance of a **major third.**

Example No. 4

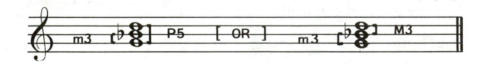

The chord symbol for a **minor triad** may be represented by one of four possible choices [min, mi, m, or –] and in each case the symbol always follows the letter name of the root tone.

Example No. 5

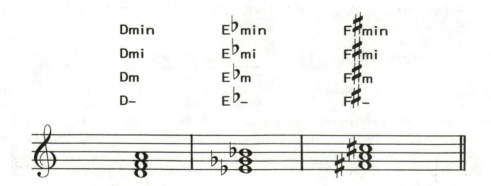

2

[3] THE AUGMENTED TRIAD

The **augmented triad** contains a **major** third and an **augmented** fifth above the root. Or, in other words, an **augmented triad** consists of two successive intervals of a third, the first interval representing the distance of a **major third** and the second interval representing the distance of an additional **major third**.

Example No. 6

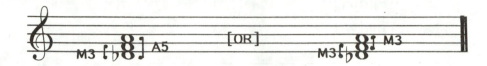

The chord symbol to express the interval of the **augmented fifth** may be shown in four different ways; (+5), (♯5), a plus sign without parentheses, or simply the abbreviation "aug" placed to the right of the letter name. In each case they all mean the same thing.

Example No. 7

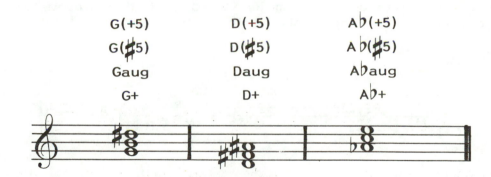

G(+5)	D(+5)	A♭(+5)
G(♯5)	D(♯5)	A♭(♯5)
Gaug	Daug	A♭aug
G+	D+	A♭+

[4] THE DIMINISHED TRIAD

The **diminished triad** contains a **minor** third and a **diminished** fifth above the root. Or, in other words, a **diminished triad** consists of two successive intervals of a third, the first interval representing the distance of a **minor third** and the second interval representing the distance of an additional **minor third**.

Example No. 8

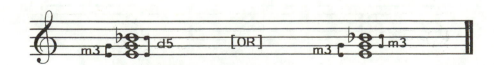

3

The chord symbol for the **diminished triad** is represented by either a small circle or the simple abbreviation "dim." In either case when using these designations, they must always be placed to the right of the letter name. Additionally, the **diminished triad** may also be designated as a **minor triad with a lowered fifth.**

Example No. 9

[5] THE MAJOR TRIAD WITH THE LOWERED FIFTH

The **major triad with the lowered fifth** contains a **major** third and a **diminished** fifth above the root tone. Or, in other words, this unique triad consists of two successive intervals of a third, the first interval representing the distance of a **major third** and the second interval representing the distance of a **diminished third.**

Example No. 10

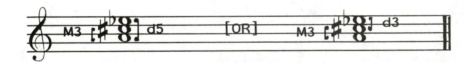

The chromatic alteration of the **lowered fifth** or the **diminished fifth** is symbolized as a (–5) or (♭5) and placed to the right of the capital letter name of the chord.

Example No. 11

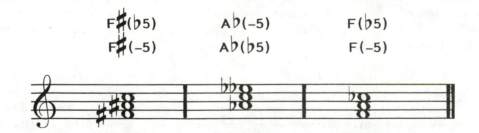

4

[6] THE SUSPENDED TRIAD

The **suspended triad** is unique in sound and is born out of contrapuntal invention. It is a major or minor triad which contains <u>no</u> interval of the third and, indeed, has substituted the interval of a fourth <u>for</u> its third. Or, in other words, this triad consists of two successive intervals, the first interval representing the distance of a **perfect fourth** and the second interval representing the distance of a **major second**.

Example No. 12

The chord symbol for the **suspended triad** is represented by the capital letter name of the chord followed by the abbreviation "sus" or "sus 4."

Example No. 13

INVERSIONS

Triads can be arranged or aligned to create what is commonly known as **inversions**. Since each triad contains three different pitches, three different alignments of the same triad are possible. That is to say, when the **root** of the triad is the lowest pitch and the third and fifth are stacked directly above in thirds, the triad is in **root position**. Additionally, when the **third** represents the lowest sound and the fifth and the root are placed directly above, the triad is in **first inversion**. And, finally, when the **fifth** is the lowest sound and the root and third are placed directly above, the triad is in **second inversion**.

Inversions in the Alphabetical Chord System are indicated by the letter name and type of triad plus the use of a slash with the letter name indicating the lowest pitch in the alignment. Occasionally, the word <u>Bass</u> is placed below the slash and directly to the right of the letter name. **Figured Bass** numbers, which will be dealt with next, are sometimes shown.

Example No. 14

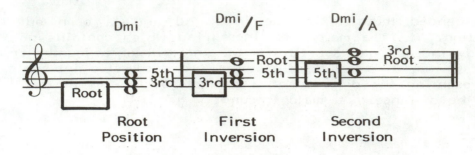

FIGURED BASS

Figured Bass -- a musical shorthand -- was widely used by composers and keyboard players of the Baroque era. Today, it is a system used almost universally as an aid in the teaching of part-writing. Different harmonies, inversions, and contrapuntal devices are indicated by the use of Arabic numerals, placed below a given bass line, to show the interval distances between the bass and upper voices.

In the following example certain Figured Bass numerals are placed in parentheses. These are numerals which are seldom given and, most often, are understood in the study of traditional harmony; therefore, in doing part-writing exercises, a given bass note without numbers placed below it is understood to be a triad in root position. Similarly, when a first inversion is wanted, only the number six is shown. In the Alphabetical Chord System, however, the first and second inversion numbers are generally placed in parentheses and given in their entirety.

Example No. 15

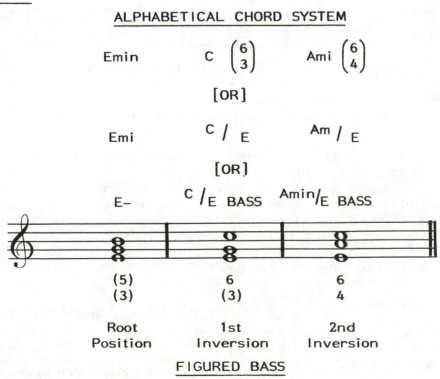

FIGURED BASS

SUGGESTED STUDY QUESTIONS

1. Define the term **triad** in music.

2. Name the **four** basic **triads**.

3. Two additional **triads** exist and are found in conjunction with seventh and, sometimes, extension chords. Name them.

4. By computing both intervals from the **root**, name the **two** intervals which comprise a **major triad**.

5. In using the Alphabetical Chord System, how does one indicate a **major triad**?

6. Is there more than **one** way to indicate a **major triad**?

7. By computing both intervals from the **root**, name the **two** intervals which comprise a **minor triad**.

8. Give at least **four** ways to indicate a **minor triad**.

9. Name the two successive intervals which comprise an **augmented triad**.

10. Give at least **four** ways to indicate an **augmented triad**.

11. Name the two successive intervals which comprise the **diminished triad**.

12. Give at least three symbols for a **diminished triad**.

13. Which interval provides the unique sound as it concerns the **major triad with the lowered fifth**?

14. Give at least two symbols for the **major triad with the lowered fifth**.

15. What makes the **suspended triad** unique?

16. How does one indicate the **suspended triad**?

17. Name the three possible alignments of any given **triad**.

18. Define the term **figured bass** in music.

19. Give at least three ways to indicate the **second inversion** in the Alphabetical Chord System.

20. What are the **figured bass** numerals for the three different alignments of any **major triad**? Which intervals are understood?

SUGGESTED KEYBOARD DRILL

1. Play each **root position triad** presented in Part I.

2. Take each **triad** presented in Part I, and play it in **root position, first inversion,** and **second inversion.**

3. Play the three triadic formulas provided below in **root position** on the following root tones: C, D, F, D♭, E♭, F♯, and B♭.

#1
Major ⌇ Major (♭5) ⌇ Major ⌇ Major (+5) ⌇ Major

#2
Major ⌇ Minor ⌇ Diminished ⌇ Minor ⌇ Major

#3
Suspended ⌇ Major ⌇ Suspended ⌇ Minor ⌇ Suspended ⌇ Major

4. Play the three triadic formulas, previously introduced, in **first inversion** on the following root tones: G, E, C♯, A♭, B, A, and G♭.

5. Play the three previously presented triadic formulas in **second inversion** on the following root tones: C♭, D♭, E♭, F♯, G, D, and C♯.

SUGGESTED EAR-TRAINING DRILL

1. Sing the following triadic formula within the architectural limits provided. Transpose it from c' to g', c♯', a♭, b, d', and a.

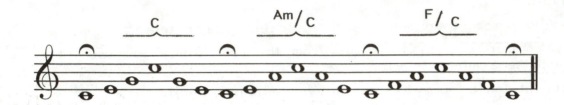

2. Make a cassette tape at the piano of various triads and their assorted alignments. Follow the graphic design presented below. The total tape time for this drill should not exceed 30 minutes. It is important that each exercise segment within the allotted time be short. This will allow for the necessary repetition and quick assimilation of the material presented. Incidentally, provide the reference pitch middle c for each exercise.

TIME SCHEMATIC & NARRATION

[Material To Be Presented]

(Announcer:)   (Announcer:)

Exercise Number One.   The answer is
The reference pitch   [Silence]   D major Triad
is middle c.   First Inversion

‖0"_____15"‖_____25"‖_____30"‖
         (15")   (10")   (5")

[Sound Material ------- Response Space ------- Taped Answer]

QUIZ #1

Identify:

1. _____ 2. _____ 3. _____ 4. _____ 5. _____ 6. _____

7. _____ 8. _____ 9. _____ 10. _____ 11. _____ 12. _____

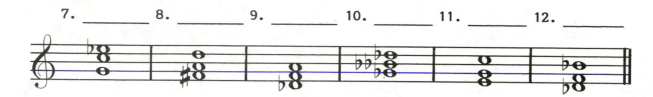

QUIZ #2

Supply:

1. F#   2. Em/B   3. B (+5)   4. G /D   5. D♭ (♭5)   6. A♭sus

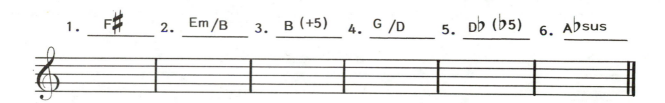

7. Dm /F   8. E♭/G   9. Fm/A♭   10. A♭/E♭   11. D♭m   12. A#°

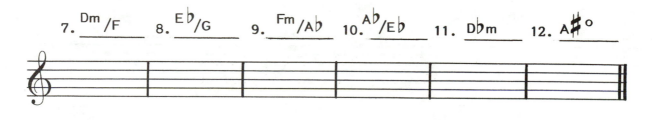

Answers to Quiz #2

1. F#A#C#   2. BEG   3. BD#Fx   4. DGB   5. D♭FA♭♭   6. A♭D♭E♭
7. FAD   8. GB♭E♭   9. A♭CF   10. E♭A♭C   11. D♭FA♭   12. A#C#E

Answers to Quiz #1

1. E   2. F#°   3. D sus4   4. Bm/D   5. G (+5)   6. A /C#
7. Cm/G   8. D /F#   9. D♭ (+5)   10. G♭m   11. C/E   12. B♭m/D♭

9

SEVENTH CHORDS

In Part I, chords were introduced at the three-note level: root, third, and fifth. In this section of the text, chords will be presented at the four-note level: root, third, fifth, and **seventh**. With the addition of this fourth tone, chords now become more complex.

There are **six** basic **seventh chord** categories; three of them have variations. Each of these chord types and variations is presented below:

[1]   the **Dominant Seventh**, its two altered fifth forms, and its unique "sus 4" alignment;

[2]   the **Major Seventh**, its more consonant seventh substitute, the Added Sixth, and its "sus 4" alignment;

[3]   the **Minor Seventh**;

[4]   the **Half-Diminished Seventh**;

[5]   the **Fully-Diminished Seventh**; and

[6]   the **Minor/Major Seventh**, its common seventh substitute, the Minor Added Sixth, and its "sus 4" alignment.

THE INTERVAL OF THE SEVENTH

On each of these chord triads is placed one of three possible **intervals of the seventh**. The **seventh**, the interval which is calculated up from the chord root, will be either an interval of a major seventh, a minor seventh, or a diminished seventh.

Example No. 16

Within the Alphabetical chord System, the **interval of the minor seventh** is <u>always</u> represented by the Arabic number **seven**. The **Added Sixth** chord, which may contain either a major or minor triad, will <u>always</u> contain an interval of a **major sixth** and <u>no</u> interval of the seventh.

Example No. 17

[1] THE DOMINANT SEVENTH

In the first category the **Dominant Seventh** chord, in its simplest form, contains two elements: a <u>major triad</u>, which is indicated by its <u>capital letter name</u>, plus a <u>minor seventh interval</u>, which is designated by the number <u>seven</u>. As was previously stated, chords containing the <u>minor seventh interval</u> are shown simply by an Arabic number <u>seven</u>; therefore, whenever the number <u>seven</u> is placed to the right of a capital letter, the number makes reference to the <u>interval of the minor seventh</u> and the <u>capital letter</u> makes reference to the <u>major triad</u>. In the following example the overall chord quality is that of a **Dominant Seventh** chord.

Example No. 18

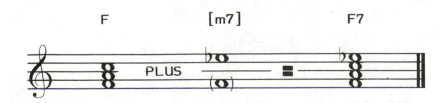

[1a] THE ALTERED DOMINANT SEVENTH

The **Altered Dominant Seventh** chord contains a triad which has either a <u>lowered</u> or <u>raised fifth</u> plus a <u>minor seventh interval</u>. Hence, there are **two Altered Dominant Seventh** chords. The preferred symbol designation is given above each chord example. Other symbol variations are also shown.

Example No. 19a

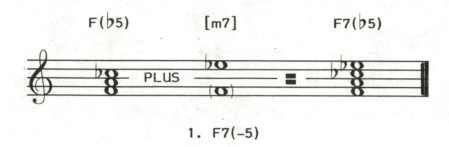

1. F7(−5)

Example No. 19b

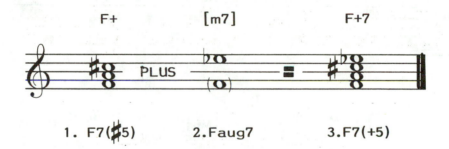

1. F7(♯5)   2. Faug7   3. F7(+5)

[1b] THE DOMINANT SEVENTH "SUS 4"

Finally, in this category the **Dominant Seventh "sus 4"** chord contains the <u>suspended triad</u>, which was encountered in Part I, plus a <u>minor seventh interval</u>. Its use is quite common today and its sound unique; moreover, it is most often considered to be a self-contained sound requiring no resolution of its suspended fourth. Once again, it is essential that the **third** of the triad be discarded when using this structure. The **third** is <u>never</u> included in the "sus 4" alignment.

Example No. 20

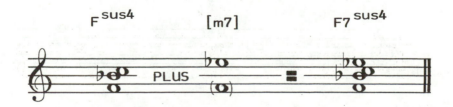

[2] THE MAJOR SEVENTH

The second, seventh chord category involves the **Major Seventh** chord. This chord type contains a major triad plus an interval of a major seventh.

Example No. 21

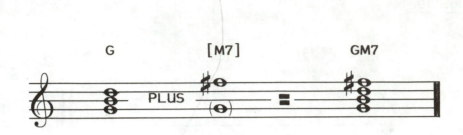

Additionally, **two** other chords exist in this category: the major triad plus the seventh substitute — the **Added Sixth** chord; and the major triad containing the suspended fourth plus the interval of the major seventh — the **Major Seventh "sus 4"** chord.

Example No. 22a

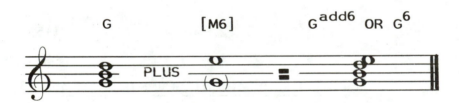

Example No. 22b

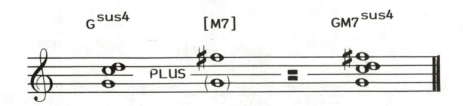

[3] THE MINOR SEVENTH

The **Minor Seventh** chord is found in the third category of seventh chords. This chord contains a <u>minor triad</u> plus an <u>interval of a minor seventh</u>. It is important to repeat, at this point, that the small letter "m" refers to the **minor triad** and not the <u>interval of the minor seventh</u>; moreover, as was previously stated, all **minor seventh** intervals are shown by the Arabic number **seven** without any modifiers.

Example No. 23

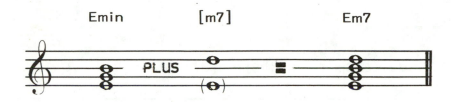

[4] THE HALF-DIMINISHED SEVENTH

The **Half-Diminished Seventh** represents the fourth category of seventh chords. It is primarily different from the previous category by virtue of its **lowered fifth**; hence, only the <u>triad is diminished</u> while the <u>interval of the minor seventh</u> remains intact. The fact that <u>only</u> half of this alignment is <u>diminished</u> accounts for the name **Half-Diminished**. In addition this chord may be symbolized in **two** different ways. It may be referred to as a <u>minor seventh, flat five</u> [Xm7(♭5)] or simply as a <u>half-diminished seventh</u> [Xø7] chord.

Example No. 24

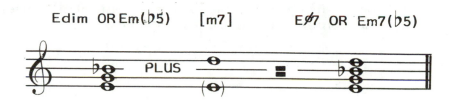

[5] THE FULLY-DIMINISHED SEVENTH

The fifth category of sevenths involves the **Fully-Diminished Seventh** chord. This chord alignment contains a <u>diminished triad</u> as well as an <u>interval of a diminished seventh</u>. The word "fully" makes reference to both component parts as being diminished. Although the <u>interval of the diminished seventh</u> is often written as a <u>major sixth</u>, the chord symbol should <u>never</u> be shown as an added sixth chord. **[See Part III of this text for a more detailed presentation of the Fully-Diminished Seventh Chord]**

Example No. 25a

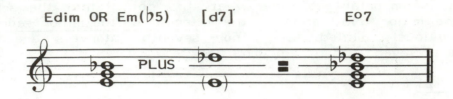

Edim OR Em(♭5)   [d7]   E°7

PLUS

Example No. 25b

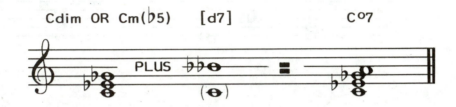

Cdim OR Cm(♭5)   [d7]   C°7

PLUS

[6] THE MINOR/MAJOR SEVENTH

The sixth and last category of sevenths is the **Minor/Major Seventh** chord and its variations. It is so described because the chord alignment contains a minor triad plus a major seventh interval. Its common seventh substitute variation contains the same minor triad but utilizes an interval of a major sixth instead of a major seventh. It is commonly referred to as the **Minor Added Sixth** chord.

The **"sus 4"** chord is in actuality the same as it was presented in category two. The only difference lies in the intent of its use, and this can only be judged by the context of the musical expression.

Example No. 26a

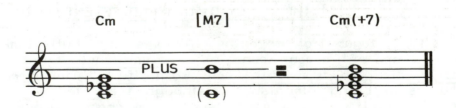

Cm   [M7]   Cm(+7)

PLUS

Example No. 26b

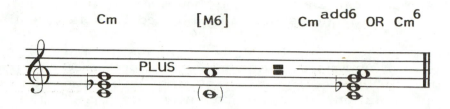

Example No. 26c

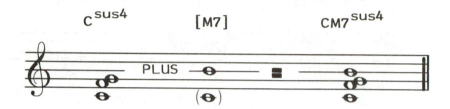

INVERSIONS

Seventh chord and triad inversions are aligned in a similar manner. The only difference between these structures lies in the additional **third inversion**. Because seventh chords represent a four-note level of alignment instead of three, a **root position** and **three inversions** are possible.

Example No. 27

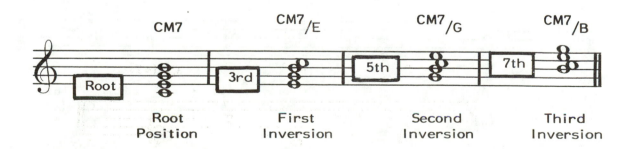

FIGURED BASS

Figured Bass numerals at the four-note level (Seventh Chords) are never seen in the Alphabetical Chord System; however, in the study of part-writing at the college level, an understanding of Figured Bass is essential.

As was encountered in the study of triads in Part I, certain Figured Bass numerals are understood and are again presented in parentheses. All other numerals are universally used and should be committed to memory. At this level of presentation, it should be understood that Figured Bass numerals are governed by the tonality in which they are found. Accidentals are shown only when using borrowed chords or melodic invention outside the intended tonality. Therefore, in the first example below which is presented in the tonality of F major, B♭ is not indicated in the Figured Bass numerals. However, had this example been presented as part of G major (2nd example), then each numeral referring to B♭ would be shown with a flat sign to the right of the number.

Example No. 28a

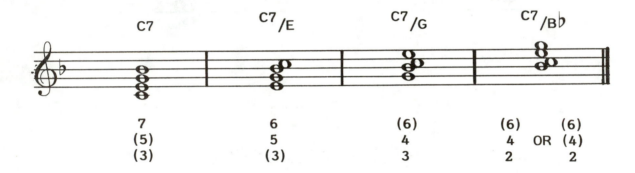

Example No. 28b

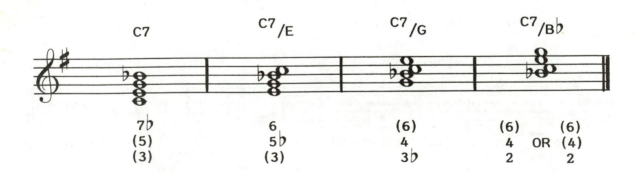

18

Additionally, lone accidentals found below a given bass note always make reference to an adjusted third above that note. Remember that bass notes may or may not be the root tone of the chord to be realized. Also, when using accidentals, it may be necessary to show those numerals which are normally not shown and understood.

Example No. 29

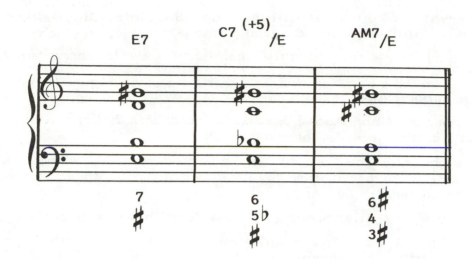

SUGGESTED STUDY QUESTIONS

1. Define and name the **six** basic seventh chords.

2. Which seventh chord types have **variations**? Name them.

3. Name **three** possible **intervals of the seventh** used with seventh chords.

4. In the Alphabetical Chord System, which Arabic number represents the **interval of the minor seventh**?

5. What is the so-called **major seventh substitute**?

6. What does the word **altered** imply as it concerns the **Dominant Seventh** chord?

7. Give at least six symbol designations for the **two altered Dominant Seventh Chords.**

8. Which pitch component is <u>always</u> discarded in the **Dominant Seventh Sus4** chord?

9. What does the capital letter "M" refer to in the **Major Seventh** chord symbol?

10. Which quality of sixth will <u>always</u> be selected for the **Added Sixth** chord?

11. What does the small letter "m" refer to in the **Em7** chord symbol?

12. What is the only structural difference between a **Fully-Diminished** and a **Half-Diminished** seventh chord?

13. Which two chord symbols are currently used to designate a **Half-Diminished** seventh chord?

14. What part of a **Half-Diminished** seventh chord is <u>diminished</u>?

15. Why is the term "<u>fully</u>" used to describe the **Fully-Diminished** seventh chord?

16. Why is it important to modify the word <u>diminished</u> when referring to specific types of seventh chords?

17. What interval is often <u>substituted</u> for the **interval of the diminished seventh** in a **Fully-Diminished** seventh chord?

18. Is it permissible to call a **Fully-Diminished** seventh chord an **Added Sixth chord?**

19. Define the **Minor/Major** seventh chord.

20. Does the phrase **Minor Added Sixth** in chord terminology make reference to the quality of the <u>interval of the sixth</u>?

21. A **Plus** sign may be placed in a chord symbol without the use of parentheses and also, at times, placed within parentheses. Does it matter? Explain the difference, if any.

22. How many different alignments are possible with seventh chords?

23. Give the **Figured Bass** inversion number(s) for a seventh chord when the **root (third, fifth,** or **seventh)** is the lowest sounding pitch in the chord alignment?

24. When are <u>accidentals</u> placed to the right of the **Figured Bass** numbers?

25. What does a <u>lone</u> accidental refer to under a given bass note when attempting to realize a **Figured Bass**?

SUGGESTED KEYBOARD DRILL

1. Play each **seventh chord** presented in Part II.

2. Take each seventh chord presented and play it in **root position, first, second,** and **third inversion.**

3. Play the <u>four</u> seventh chord formulas provided below, in **root position** on the following chord roots: C, C♯/D♭, D, E♭, E, F, F♯/G♭, G, A♭, A, B♭, and B.

#1

XM7 〰 X7 〰 X^6

#2

Xm(+7) 〰 Xm7 〰 Xm^6

#3

XM7 〰 X7 〰 Xm7 〰 $X^{\emptyset}7$ 〰 $X^{o}7$

#4

$X7^{(+5)}$ 〰 X7 〰 $X7^{(\flat5)}$ 〰 X7 〰 $X7^{(+5)}$

4. Play the <u>three</u> sus4 formulas provided below in **root position** on the following chord roots: C, D♭, D, E♭, E, F, G♭, G, A♭, A, B♭, and B.

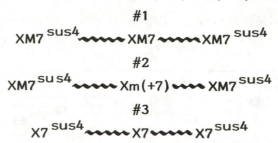

#1
XM7 ^{sus4} ～～ XM7 ～～ XM7 ^{sus4}

#2
XM7 ^{sus4} ～～ Xm (+7) ～～ XM7 ^{sus4}

#3
X7 ^{sus4} ～～ X7 ～～ X7 ^{sus4}

5. Play the previously introduced <u>root position</u> formulas in **first, second,** and **third inversion.** As you play through these formulas, evaluate each sound for its most effective voicing alignment.

SUGGESTED EAR-TRAINING DRILL

1. Sing the following **root position** chord set within the architectual limits provided. [See Part V for additional sets]

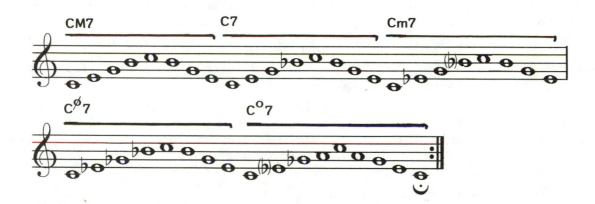

2. Sing the following chord set in **first inversion.** [See Part V for additional sets]

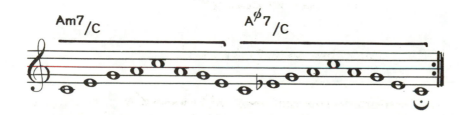

3. Sing the following chord set in **second inversion.** [See Part V for additional sets]

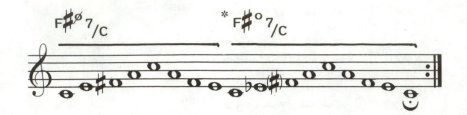

4. Sing the following chord set in **third inversion.** [See Part V for additional sets]

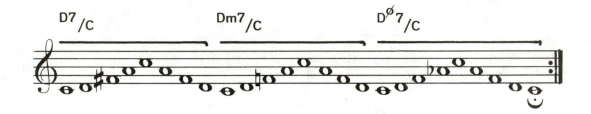

5. Refer to Page 8 of Part I, and again make a cassette tape utilizing **seventh chords** instead of triads. Be sure that your total tape time does not exceed 30 minutes.

6. Make a cassette tape of each **root position, first, second,** and **third inversion** seventh chord set previously introduced. Leave a 20" space on your tape to accomodate your verbal response plus the taped answer to each set. Throughout the tape, begin each set with <u>middle c</u> as your reference pitch.

---

* Inversions of **Fully-Diminished** chords are, at best, problematical. Its use here is for clarity of instruction. See **Part III** for more detailed information concerning **Fully-Diminished** seventh chords.

QUIZ #1

Identify:

1. _____ 2. _____ 3. _____ 4. _____ 5. _____ 6. _____

7. _____ 8. _____ 9. _____ 10. _____ 11. _____ 12. _____

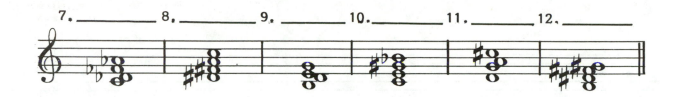

QUIZ #2

Supply:

1. A⌀7/E♭ 2. G♭7 (−5) 3. Cm7/B♭ 4. B⌀7/D 5. D♭6 6. F♯7

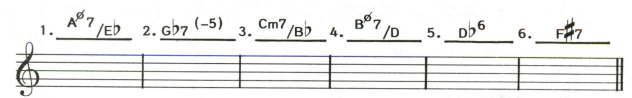

7. E♭7sus4 8. E♭m7/G♭ 9. D♭M7/F 10. F♯⌀7 11. G°7 12. B7 (+5)

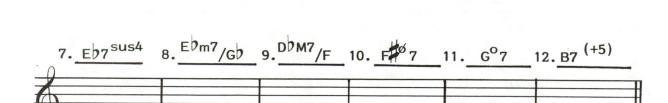

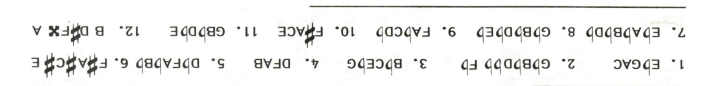

P A R T   III

EXTENSIONS

Understanding the overall concept of chordal **extensions** is predicated upon a thorough knowledge of **seventh chords**, for it is the quality of <u>both</u> the **triad** and the **interval of the seventh** which determines and/or supports the choice of one or more **extensions**.

Chordal **extensions** are grouped according to their interval size and quality. **Ninths** and **elevenths** share the potential for <u>alteration</u> while the **thirteenth** -- although sometimes, erroneously seen as an altered extension -- is presented in its traditionally <u>unaltered</u> state. By selectively combining the assorted **intervals of extension** with specific chord categories, various **ninth, eleventh,** and **thirteenth** chords can be formulated.

For the purposes of quick assimulation and visual recall, **extension sizes** and **qualities** are graphically presented -- shaped in pyramid form -- immediately below.

Example No. 30

CHORDAL IDENTIFICATION

In the utilization of chordal extensions, <u>seventh chords</u> are identified according to their **quality** and **scale degree position**. This identification allows for the reduction of hundreds of chords into a workable reservoir of **five** chord categories. This means that chords of similar construction and different scale degrees will be grouped under the strongest scale degree function within their tonal environment. For example, **Major Seventh** chord qualities are found on the **first** and **fourth** degrees in a major key scheme and, as such, are grouped together into one category. Moreover, whatever can be said for the <u>tonic</u> seventh chord can also be said for the <u>subdominant</u>, and since the <u>tonic</u> degree is stronger than the <u>subdominant</u>, both are grouped under the **I–Major Tonality** category. Similarily, **Minor Seventh** chord qualities are found in a <u>major</u> tonality on the **second, third,** and **sixth** degrees. Again, in a similar manner, these three seventh chords are then grouped under the **II–Major Tonality** category. Continuing in the same fashion, the three remaining categories are realized. The ultimate grouping of **five** categories is not unlike the <u>six</u> basic seventh chord groups previously seen in **Part II.** However, one important exception does exist, and it is the non-inclusion of the **Fully–Diminished** seventh chord category.

For the purposes of this study concerning the use of chordal **extensions,** <u>seventh chords</u> are now grouped into **five** basic categories. Every effort should be made to memorize the following information.

THE FIVE BASIC CHORDAL EXTENSION CATEGORIES

SEVENTH CHORD CATEGORY	CATEGORY ABBREVIATION	CHORD(S) OF SIMILAR CONSTRUCTION WITHIN THE MAJOR TONALITY	SEVENTH CHORD QUALITIES
1. I–MAJOR TONALITY	[I–M]	(I7) & IV7	XM7 & X^{add6}
2. I–MINOR TONALITY (MEL.)	[I–m]	NONE	Xm7(+7) & Xm^{add6}
3. II–MAJOR TONALITY	[II–M]	(II7), III7, & VI7	Xm7
4. II–MINOR TONALITY (NAT.)(HAR.)	[II–m]	$VII^{\emptyset}7$	$Xm7^{(\flat 5)}$ $(X^{\emptyset}7)$
5. V–MAJOR/MINOR TONALITY (HAR.)(MEL.)	[V]	(V7)	X7

MINOR SCALE FORMS

(NAT.)=NATURAL   (HAR.)=HARMONIC   (MEL.)=MELODIC

1. I–MAJOR TONALITY

The **I–Major Tonality** [**I–M**] chord category will support only the following extensions: the **major ninth**, the **augmented eleventh**, and the **major thirteenth**. All other intervals are not recommended. It is important to emphasize that the interval of the perfect eleventh is not used even though it is found in the tonality of the **I–M** chord category. The reason for its nonuse is that it forms the critical minor ninth interval between itself and the major third of the basic triad. This so-called "crowding" of the triad's color tone should be avoided. However, when the scale degree of the perfect eleventh is used in the sus4 alignment, it is entirely acceptable, for the third of the triad has been discarded and the troublesome interval of the minor ninth is not even a consideration. To experience what is meant by "crowding," play at the piano, in contrasting fashion, the sharp dissonance of the perfect eleventh and the recommended interval of the augmented eleventh in conjunction with the major triad. This simple experiment should prove helpful in understanding the selection process of interval extensions.

Four very important explanations, at this point, are needed to further understand chord symbols in the study of **chordal extensions**.

1. The Arabic number of the highest unaltered extension (**major ninth, perfect eleventh, & major thirteenth**) is always shown to the right of the chord letter name and not in parentheses.

2. Any extension interval altered from its **major** or **perfect** state must be placed in parentheses.

3. Numbers placed in parentheses are generally ranked from the highest to the lowest number starting from the top down.

4. All **I–M** six-nine chords are always shown in this fashion [6/9] and never include the interval of the major seventh; moreover, six-nine chords never extend beyond the interval of the **ninth**.

Example No. 31a

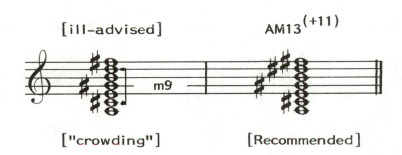

Example No. 31b

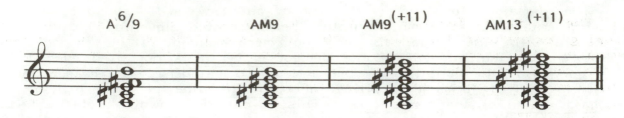

$A^{6}/_{9}$ AM9 AM9$^{(+11)}$ AM13$^{(+11)}$

2. I–MINOR TONALITY

The **I–Minor Tonality** [I–m] chord category will support the following extensions: the **major ninth**, the **perfect eleventh**, and the **major thirteenth**. However, because of chordal distortion, extensions beyond the **major ninth** are rarely seen in the I–m chord category.* The <u>diminished fifth</u>, for instance, created by the <u>major seventh</u> and the <u>perfect eleventh</u> clearly illustrates this point. Players tend to "soften" the problem of distortion by the use of the **augmented eleventh** but <u>only when the major thirteenth is included in the alignment</u>. This remedy is frequently seen when chords are utilized in a <u>polytonal</u> manner. **Polychordal** alignments will be examined later in this section.

Example No. 32a

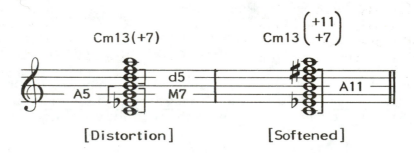

Cm13(+7)   Cm13$\left(\begin{smallmatrix}+11\\+7\end{smallmatrix}\right)$

[Distortion]   [Softened]

Example No. 32b

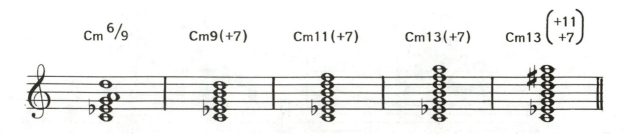

Cm$^{6}/_{9}$ Cm9(+7)   Cm11(+7)   Cm13(+7)   Cm13$\left(\begin{smallmatrix}+11\\+7\end{smallmatrix}\right)$

---

*The degree of chordal **distortion** is based upon how many <u>articulated partials</u> exist in the specific <u>Overtone Series</u> from which the chord is formulated. [SEE PART V FOR MORE DETAILS CONCERNING THE OVERTONE SERIES]

3. II—MAJOR TONALITY

The **II—Major Tonality [II—M]** chord category will support only the following extensions: the **major ninth**, the **perfect eleventh**, and the **major thirteenth**. All other intervals are <u>not</u> recommended. This chord category is by far the simplest to memorize, for each alignment reflects its home key -- found a <u>major second below</u> its chord root -- exclusively.

Example No. 33

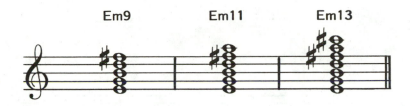

4. II—MINOR TONALITY

Although the **II—m** chord category is taken from the <u>natural</u> scale form of the minor tonality, the <u>minor ninth</u> and the <u>minor thirteenth</u> of the key are not used. When utilizing extensions for this category, the **major ninth** and the **major thirteenth** are borrowed from the <u>parallel major</u>; therefore, the **II—m** chord category will only support the following intervals: the **major ninth**, the **perfect eleventh**, and the **major thirteenth**. All other intervals are <u>not</u> recommended.

Example No. 34

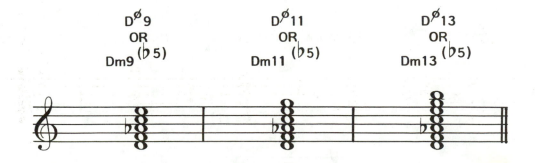

5. V—MAJOR/MINOR TONALITY

The single, and without a doubt, most versatile chord group is the **Dominant [V]** chord category. It will support <u>all</u> of the **extension intervals** with the exception of one -- the <u>perfect eleventh</u>. This interval -- as was previously shown -- causes the <u>"crowding"</u> of the triad's major third and, as such, should be avoided. Although the **Dominant Eleventh chord [X11]** is occasionally encountered, it is customary for players to sound this chord without the third of the triad present. This problem area is best solved by restricting the use of the <u>perfect eleventh</u> to that of the <u>perfect fourth</u> in the **sus4** alignment and, thereby, eliminating the problem altogether.

Example No. 35a

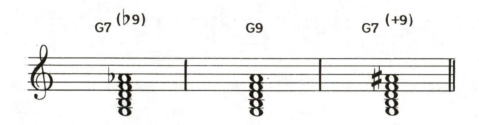

Example No. 35b

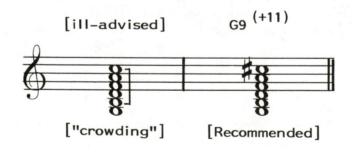

Example No. 35c

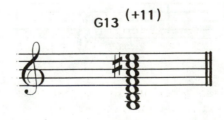

30

In addition to the **Dominant** [V] chords already introduced, several other variations exist. These are made possible by omitting one or two extensions in favor of the remaining one(s); or by altering one or several notes of the entire chord; or, simply, by combining each of the previous methods of variation. In the following example several additional chords are presented for examination and study. No attempt is made to exhaust all of the possible chordal combinations utilized by today's enterprizing musicians.

Example No. 36

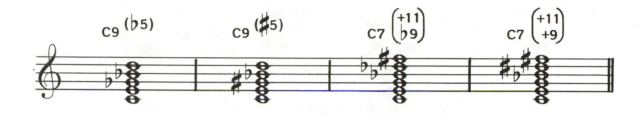

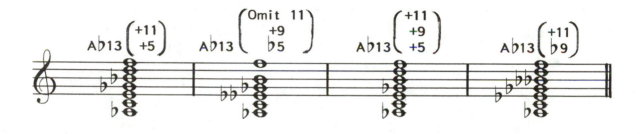

SUMMARY

The following informational chart summarizes all of what has been written so far concerning chord categories and the use of specific interval extensions. Columns one and two need no explanation; however, column three is presented solely to suggest some of the possible symbol designations which are seen in the particular chord category under examination. Also, as before, the "X" in each symbol designation is to represent any of the possible letter names utilized in the musical alphabet. Every effort should be made to study and memorize all of the material presented.

SUMMATION CHART
FOR
CHORDAL EXTENSIONS

THE CHORD CATEGORIES	INTERVAL(S) OF EXTENSION	POSSIBLE CHORD SYMBOLS
I–M		$XM9$; $X^6/9$
I–m		$Xm9(+7)$; $Xm^6/9$
II–M	[M9]	$Xm9$
II–m		$Xm9^{(\flat 5)}$ or $X^{\o}9$
V		$X9$; $X9^{(\flat 5)}$; $X9^{(+5)}$
V	[m9] or [A9]	$X7^{(\flat 9)}$; $X7^{(+9)}$
I–m		$Xm11(+7)$
II–M	[P11]	$Xm11$
II–m		$Xm11^{(\flat 5)}$ or $X^{\o}11$
I–M	[A11]	$XM9^{(+11)}$
V		$X9^{(+11)}$
I–M		$XM13^{(+11)}$
I–m		$Xm13\binom{+11}{+7}$
II–M	[M13]	$Xm13$
II–m		$Xm13^{(\flat 5)}$ or $X^{\o}13$
V		$X13^{(+11)}$

THE BRIDGING CHORD GROUP

THE FULLY-DIMINISHED SEVENTH CHORD

As was stated earlier, the **Fully-Diminished Seventh Chord** is not to be considered as part of the extension chord categories previously introduced but, rather, as a group of chords which function individually as a "bridging" or connecting device when found with various other chord categories in an harmonic progression. Rhythmically, the **Fully-Diminished Seventh chord** is found, most often, on weak beats or fractions of beats within a musical context. Because of its many peculiarities, the **Fully-Diminished Seventh Chord** requires special consideration in the study of chords.

Since **Fully-Diminished Seventh Chords** are comprised of a series of minor thirds, they never extend, theoretically, beyond the four-note level. A fourth minor third placed above the diminished seventh interval would simply reiterate the root tone of the chord; therefore, chordal extensions such as ninths, elevenths, and thirteenths do not exist by definition.

Example No. 37

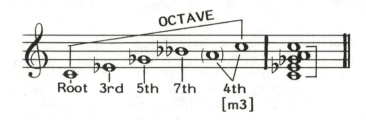

It is possible, however, to indicate various non-harmonic tones above the root, third, and occasionally the fifth of the **Fully-Diminished Seventh Chord**. In each case the desired pitch or pitches must represent a distance of a major ninth above the designated chord tone and, necessarily, involve one letter change. This method allows the composer, arranger, or performer a broader capability with so-called "bridging" chords and, at the same time, utilizes a method which does not contradict the tertiary system of chordal construction. It should be understood that at no time are these letter names referred to as chordal extensions.

Example No. 38

Single or double appoggiaturas -- non-harmonic tones used in the place of chord member tones -- may be utilized with "bridging" chords. It is important to remember that the chord tone(s) being replaced is seldom, if ever, played simultaneously with the **appoggiatura** note(s).

Example No. 39

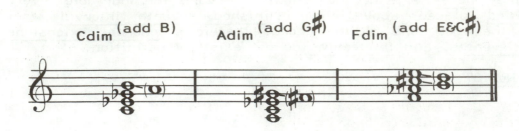

Cdim (add B)   Adim (add G♯)   Fdim (add E&C♯)

Because the **Fully-Diminished Seventh Chord** equally divides the octave, each chord tone is equally important. Or, in other words, no one chord tone is more prominent than another. The importance of this concept is that each chord tone or its enharmonic equivalent may now function as a root tone thereby allowing each **Fully-Diminished Seventh Chord** four possible root names. The appropriate identification of a **Fully-Diminished Seventh Chord** can only be determined in a thorough study of the context in which it appears.

Example No. 40

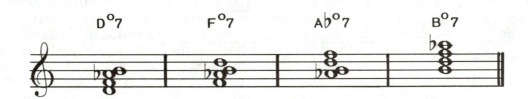

D°7   F°7   A♭°7   B°7

Additionally, the equal division of the octave allows yet another interesting aspect of **Fully-Diminished Seventh Chords**. Since each chord is now capable of having four possible roots and since there are twelve pitches in an octave, there can be only three possible **Fully-Diminished Seventh Chords**. All other **Fully-Diminished Seventh Chords** are merely enharmonic spellings of the three basic chords presented immediately below.

Example No. 41

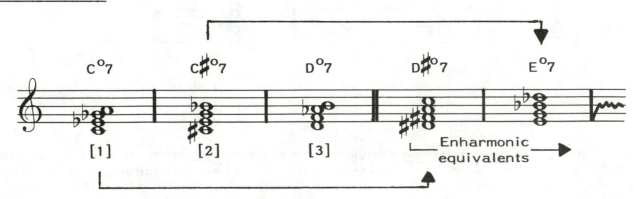

C°7   C♯°7   D°7   D♯°7   E°7

[1]   [2]   [3]

Enharmonic equivalents

34

Finally, the writing of **Fully-Diminished Seventh Chords** requires some attention. If one merely avoids writing double flats ($\flat\flat$) and the troublesome pitches of <u>F-flat</u> and <u>C-flat</u>, all **Fully-Diminished Seventh Chords** will become quite easy to write and to identify. In addition a good 'rule of thumb' is to choose sharp and natural pitches as chord roots and to avoid flats whenever possible; however, on some occasions flats are given as root tones and must be dealt with. In the following example several varities of **Fully-Diminished Seventh Chords** are presented to provide a clearer representation of possible enharmonic adjustments. No attempt is made to present each and every possible **Fully-Diminished Seventh Chord.**

Example No. 42

THE COMPOUND CHORD SYMBOL

Compound chord symbols are used to designate very complex or highly altered chords regardless of their harmonic validity. The symbol, itself, is characterized by a **slashed diagonal line** which usually indicates a <u>seventh chord</u> structure to the **left** of the **slash** and a <u>single bass note</u> to the **right**. For example, the symbol E♭m7/C (E-flat Minor Seventh over a C Bass) simply denotes that the chord to the **left** of the **slash** will consist of **E-flat**, **G-flat**, **B-flat**, and **D-flat** and that the note to the **right** of the **slash** will be **C.**

Example No. 43

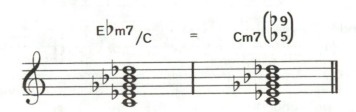

Chords of special effect which do not conform to the <u>Five Basic Chordal</u> <u>Extension Categories</u> -- such as the I-M, I-m, II-M, or II-m <u>flat ninth chords</u> -- are best designated as **compound chords** or **polychordal** alignments. The <u>flat ninth interval</u> above these chord categories would not be considered a logical or traditional extension. Ease of reading and recognition may also involve the redefining of enharmonic spellings of complex and altered chords. These chords may be written in an optional manner. It should be emphasized that this optional technique should not be abused in redefining chord symbols pertaining to the <u>Five Basic Chordal Extension Categories</u>.

Example No. 44

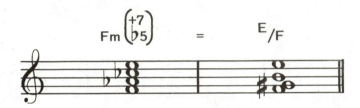

As we have previously seen in **Part I & II**, **compound chord symbols** may be used to describe <u>triadic inversions</u> and <u>inversions involving larger</u> <u>alignments</u>. Chord progressions which are involved with the technique of **Organ Point** -- often referred to as **Pedal Point** -- may also utilize the system of **compound chord symbols**.

Example No. 45

THE POLYCHORDAL SYMBOL

The **polychordal symbol** is characterized by a <u>short horizontal line</u> separating <u>two</u> clearly defined chord symbols. Its utilization serves to clarify highly altered, and often complex, six-and seven-part chords with a symbol of greater readability. As with the <u>compound chord symbol</u>, harmonic validity of **polychordal** alignments is not essential. Although primarily adaptable to <u>polytonal</u> contexts, **polychordal** alignments may be used in singular tonal contexts.

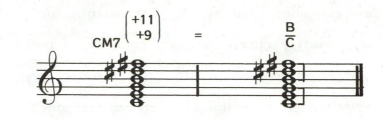

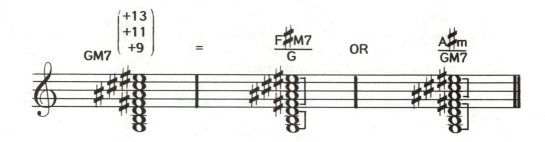

SUGGESTED STUDY QUESTIONS

1. Why is it important to know the quality of the **triad** and the **interval of the seventh** in the selection of extensions?

2. Which interval sizes are considered **extensions**?

3. Why were **extensions** graphically presented in the shape of a pyramid?

4. Name the **Five Basic Chordal Extension Categories.**

5. Which chord group is not considered part of the **Five Basic Chordal Extension Categories**?

6. What is meant by the designation **I-M**?

7. Which **extensions** are recommended for use in the **I-M Tonality** category?

8. Why is it not necessary to use any modifiers in the **6/9** chord symbol?

9. What is the main difference between the **I-M** and **I-m** chord categories?

10. Does the capital "M" in the **II-M** designation mean that the **II** chord is **major**? If not, what does it signify?

11. What is meant by "crowding" and how is it associated with the minor ninth interval?

12. Would the chord symbol **Gm11/C** avoid the ill-advised minor ninth in the **C11** chord?

13. What kind of Arabic numbers are placed in parentheses?

14. Which **extensions** are supported by the **I-m** designation?

15. Why is the **II-M Tonality** chord category so easy to memorize?

16. Which **extensions** are supported by the **II-M Tonality** chord category?

17. How does the **II-M** differ from the **II-m** chord category?

18. How does one avoid "crowding" in the writing of **Dominant Eleventh** chords?

19. What chord category is the most versatile and for what reason?

20. What kind of chord group is considered "bridging?"

21. Why do **ninths, elevenths,** and **thirteenths** not exist on **Fully-Diminished Seventh Chords?**

22. When are letter names placed in parentheses in a chord symbol?

23. What's the meaning of the term **appoggitura?**

24. Explain why it is possible to have <u>four</u> possible root names for a **Fully-Diminished Seventh Chord?**

25. How many <u>basic</u> **Fully-Diminished Seventh Chords** are possible?

26. What types of accidentals should be avoided in the writing of **Fully-Diminished Seventh Chords?**

27. For what reasons are **compound** chord symbols formulated?

28. The <u>slashed diagonal line</u> and the <u>short horizontal line</u> are both used in the Alphabetical Chord System. For what purpose is each of them used?

29. Why is it sometimes necessary to use **polychordal** alignments?

30. What is meant by the expression, "chords of special effect?"

SUGGESTED KEYBOARD DRILL

1. Play each chord presented in **Part III** and attempt to understand the aural sense of each example given.

2. Play each category of chords and attempt to separate them aurally.

3. Reproduce at the piano each chord category presented in the "**Summation Chart For Chordal Extensions**" (**See Page 32**) in as many different key signatures, as possible.

4. Formulate and play as many **Fully–Diminished Seventh Chords** on white-keyed roots as well as sharped black-keyed roots, as possible.

5. Attempt to aurally understand the use of the **appoggitura** concept as it relates to diminished triads.

6. Formulate and name as you play -- without the aid of paper and pencil -- as many **compound** chords, as possible.

7. Formulate and name as you play -- without the aid of paper and pencil -- as many **polychordal** alignments, as possible.

SUGGESTED EAR–TRAINING DRILL

For each chord category, primary and secondary scale studies have been provided. While singing each drill, try to develop an aural awareness for each chord identity, its extensions, and its given primary or secondary scale.

1. **I–M Tonality:** a) Sing the following **Lydian** mode within the architectual limits provided. The **Lydian** mode is the primary scale for the following **I–M** chords: **C6; CM7; C6/9; CM9(+11); & CM13(+11).** [See Part V for a complete listing of Modal scales]

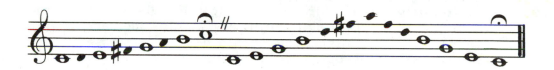

b) The **Ionian** mode may be used as a secondary scale for the following chords: **C6; CM7; C6/9; & CM9.** Its use as a primary scale is best confined to the **CM9sus4** chord.

2. **I–m Tonality:** a) Sing the following **Melodic Minor** scale within the architectual limits provided. The **Melodic Minor** scale (primary) and the **Harmonic Minor** scale (secondary) are used with all **I–m** chords containing a raised seventh. The **Melodic Minor** scale may also function as a primary scale for the following **I–m** chords: **Cm6; & Cm6/9.**

b) The **Dorian** mode is the primary scale for the following I-m chords: **Cm6; Cm7; Cm6/9; Cm11; & Cm13.** It is important to note the inclusion of the <u>major sixth</u> and <u>minor seventh</u> intervals in this scale choice.

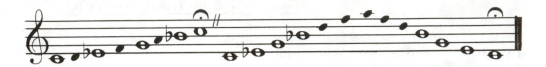

3. II-M Tonality: a) See Drill Study 2b of the I-m **Tonality** category. The determination of scale degree function between **I-m** and **II-M** chord categories can only be realized through an understanding of the context. The following **II-M** chords relate directly to the primary **Dorian** mode: **Cm7; Cm9; Cm11; & Cm13.**

4. II-m Tonality: a) Sing the following displaced **Harmonic major** scale of B♭ major placed within the architectual limits provided. This scale contains the necessary pitches to fulfill the requirements of the **triad**, the **seventh**, and the borrowed **extensions** of the <u>parallel major</u>. It becomes the primary scale for this category. The usual choice for a **Half-Diminished** <u>Seventh</u> **Chord** is the **Locrian** mode. The following chords relate directly to the displaced **Harmonic major** scale: **Cm9(♭5); Cm11(♭5); & Cm13(♭5).**

5. V-M/m Tonality: a) Sing the following **Lydian Dominant** mode placed within the architectual limits provided. This primary scale relates directly to the following **Dominant** chords: **C7; C9; C9(+11); & C13(+11).**

b) The **Mixolydian** mode is usually chosen for the following **Dominant** chords: C7sus; C7; C9sus; C11[Gm7/C]; & C13[Gm9/C].

c) Sing the following primary **Diminished** scale $[\frac{1}{2}-W]$ placed within the architectual limits provided. This scale relates directly to the following **Dominant** chords: C7($\flat$9); C7(+9); C13(+9&+11); & C13($\flat$9&+11).

d) For **altered fifths** the primary **Whole-tone** scale relates directly to the following **Dominant** chords: C7(+5); C7($\flat$5); C9(+5); & C9($\flat$5).

6. <u>**Fully-Diminished**</u> a) Sing the following primary **Diminished** scale $[W-\frac{1}{2}]$
   <u>**Seventh Chord:**</u> placed within the architectual limits provided.

7. Refer to Page 8 of Part I, and again make a cassette tape utilizing chords with **extensions**. Be sure that your total tape time does not exceed 30 minutes. All chords should be sounded in an arpeggio fashion as well as in a blocked vertical manner.

QUIZ #1

Identify:

1. _____ 2. _____ 3. _____ 4. _____ 5. _____ 6. _____

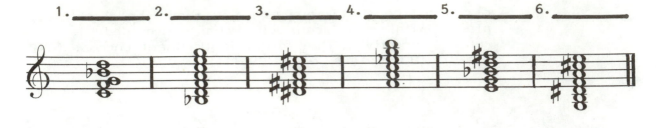

7. _____ 8. _____ 9. _____ 10. _____ 11. _____ 12. _____

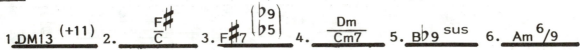

QUIZ #2

Supply:

1. DM13 $^{(+11)}$ 2. $\dfrac{F\sharp}{C}$ 3. F$\sharp$7 $\binom{\flat 9}{\flat 5}$ 4. $\dfrac{Dm}{Cm7}$ 5. B$\flat$9 ^{sus} 6. Am $^{6}/9$

7. B $^{6}/9$ 8. $\dfrac{E\flat m7}{C}$ 9. B$\flat$13 $^{(+11)}$ 10. A7 $^{(+9)}$ 11. $\dfrac{Fm ^{(+7)}}{G}$ 12. E$\flat^{\emptyset}$7/A$\flat$

Section 1

CHORD PROGRESSION

The theory of **chord progression** is governed primarily by a "linear" process involving, in part, what is referred to as root movement. It is a process which involves the treatment and resolution of dissonant intervals and the melodic movement of root relationships between chords.

To more graphically describe this process, two sets of examples have been provided. In the first set note carefully **a)** the treatment and resolution of each dissonant minor seventh interval, **b)** the primary movement (distance) of root relationships between chords, **c)** the three axes -- that upon which the "linear" progressions pivot -- and, **c)** the implied new harmony sounded in the chord of resolution. Although the implied new harmony in each example is major, minor chords of resolution are possible, as well. It should be understood that the minor seventh interval, unlike the major seventh, cannot satisfactorily be resolved within its own harmony and, therefore, needs and demands a new chord of resolution. It is this specific "linear" process in the treatment of the dissonant minor seventh interval which establishes and generates harmonic movement.

Example No. 47a

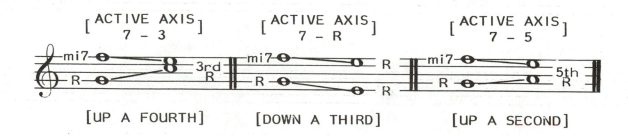

In addition to <u>primary</u> root movements there are three <u>secondary</u> root movements. They are <u>referred</u> to as <u>secondary</u> because of the passive nature of the treatment and resolution of the <u>minor seventh interval</u>.

In the second set note carefully **a)** the treatment and resolution of each dissonant <u>minor seventh interval</u>, **b)** the <u>secondary</u> movement (distance) of root relationships between chords, **c)** the <u>three axes</u> -- that upon which the "linear" progressions pivot -- and, **d)** the implied <u>new</u> harmony sounded in the chord of resolution.

<u>Example No. 47b</u>

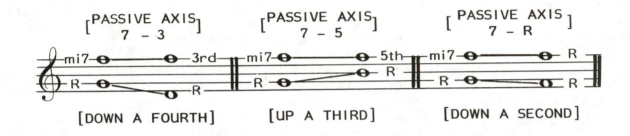

When involving the treatment and resolution of the <u>minor seventh interval</u>, only <u>six</u> root movements are possible: <u>three primary</u> and <u>three secondary</u>. Each is characterized by its relative function and strength. Also, interval sizes (distances) of root movements are not specific. For example, <u>up a fourth</u> could imply a perfect fourth or, for that matter, an augmented fourth. This freedom of choice allows for the free interchangeability of tonal centers.

Finally, two companion concepts of the "linear" process remain. The first involves the <u>tonic degree</u> and its unrestricted freedom of root movement. Any progression involving the <u>tonic</u> root is to be considered strong and desirable. <u>Primary</u> and <u>secondary</u> root movements do not apply.

The second concept involves the <u>chromatic</u> movement of roots. Any <u>chromatic</u> movement is to be encouraged and considered desirable.

The informational chart on the following page outlines all of what has been said regarding the grand concept of **chord progression**.

CHORD PROGRESSION INFORMATIONAL CHART

ROOT MOVEMENT	INTERVAL DISTANCE	COMMENTS
I–Primary	Up 4	Very strong and most common.
[Active Resolution Axes]	Down 3	Lacks contrast and demands special placement within the measure.
	Up 2	Very strong contrast and clear forward motion.
II–Secondary	Down 4	Lacks stability and is considered retrogressive.
[Passive Resolution Axes]	Up 3	Lacks contrast and is least used.
	Down 2	Retrogressive in quality and heard in blues.
III–Tonic	N/A	Any progression will be strong and desirable from the tonic.
IV–Chromatic	N/A	All chromatic progressions are desirable and should be encouraged.

Patterns of Chordal Progressions

Study the following chordal progressions. Each pattern contains an explanation concerning root movement and the treatment of dissonant intervals.

1.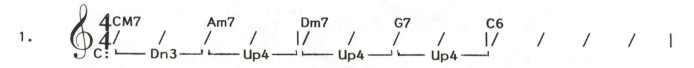

1. Each chord set root movement is of the primary variety.

2. Each minor seventh interval is resolved down to its chord of resolution utilizing the 7 to 3 axis.

3. The major seventh interval of the CM7 chord may resolve up to "c" or down to "a" of the Am7 chord.

4. The entire harmonic expression is heard in the tonality of **C major** and represents the often used harmonic formula of I–VI–II–V–I.

2.

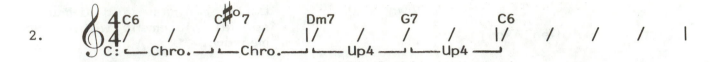

1. Two chord sets utilize <u>chromatic</u> root movement, while the cadential set progression (II–V–I) uses the <u>primary</u> variety.

2. Within the <u>primary</u> set progressions, each <u>minor seventh interval</u> resolves down to its chord of resolution utilizing the **7 to 3** axis.

3. The entire harmonic expression is heard in the tonality of **C major** with exception of the temporary feeling of **D minor** on the first beat of the second measure.

4. The cadential set progression of **Dm7** to **G7** to **C6** represents the most common harmonic formula of II–V–I.

3.

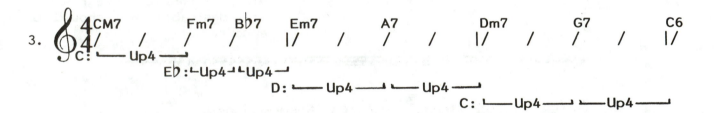

1. Each chord set root movement is of the <u>primary</u> variety.

2. Each <u>minor seventh interval</u> is resolved down to its chord of resolution utilizing the **7 to 3** axis.

3. The <u>major seventh interval</u> of the **CM7** chord may resolve up to "c" or down to "a♭" of the **Fm7** chord. Its resolution is not as critical as the <u>interval of the minor seventh</u>.

4. The non-specific nature of root movements allows the shifting of tonal centers throughout the harmonic expression.

5. The chord symbols shown are normally found as individual chord members of the tonalities indicated.

4.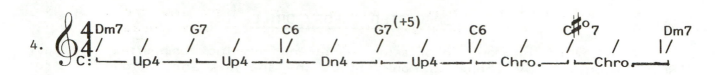

1. The majority of root movement chord sets are of the <u>primary</u> variety.

2. Each <u>minor seventh interval</u> is resolved down to its chord of resolution utilizing the **7** to **3** axis.

3. One chord set utilizes a <u>secondary</u> root movement which, coincidentally, involves movement <u>from</u> the tonic (**I**) chord.

4. Two chord sets utilize the <u>chromatic</u> method for root movement.

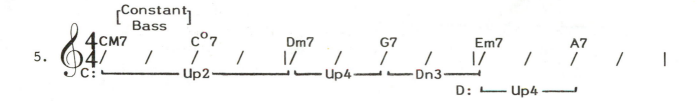

1. Each root movement chord set is of the <u>primary</u> variety with the exception of the **constant roots** of the first measure.

2. Each <u>minor seventh interval</u> is resolved down to its chord of resolution utilizing the **7** to **3** axis.

3. Some music theorists feel that the **Fully-Diminished Seventh** chord is an altered variety of a chord formulated on the <u>lowered</u> sixth degree of the grand key. Although it may somewhat function in that fashion, in this instance the composer's intent is to maintain a **constant bass**. Its main thrust is to provide some <u>chromatic</u> inner voice movement between the **CM7** and the **Dm7** chords.

4. The first two measures represent a variation of the **I-VI-II-V harmonic formula.**

5. Measure three represents a tonal shift to the key of **D major.**

SUGGESTED THEORY DRILL

1. The following harmonic expression is taken from the composition entitled, **"Round Midnight"** by **Thelonius Monk.** Study the analysis and then analyze for yourself ten other compositions of your choice. Attempt to do them in the same manner as the example.

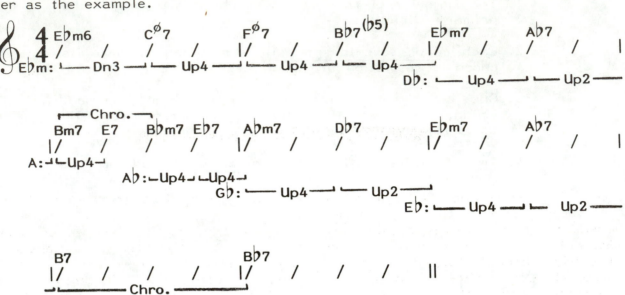

Section 2

CHORDAL DEGREE IDENTIFICATION

The importance of **chordal degree identification** is three-fold. To begin, it is necessary to assign Roman numerals to each chordal degree. This assures quick identification when working with the tonal environment. Secondly, the pinpointing of chordal degrees by Roman numerals helps identify chordal function and tendency. Lastly, through the use of Roman numeral designations and the functional identification of chordal degrees, concepts of chordal substitution become easier to understand and use.

In the following **major** key scheme, study each seventh chord presented. Attempt to associate chordal qualities with their respective Roman numeral designations. Also, notice that chord roots which are located a third apart will have three notes in common. This is the basis for chordal substitution involving common tones; this concept will be discussed in the next section of this text.

Example No. 48

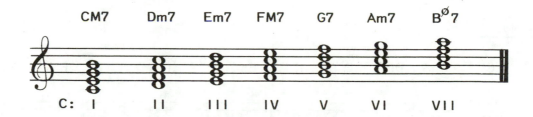

51

The **minor** key scheme poses some problems. Because of the three scale forms utilized [**natural, harmonic, & melodic**], a composite chordal scheme is presented. Again, as in the previous example, attempt to associate the chordal qualities with their respective Roman numerals and, of course, the scale forms from which each chord is derived.

Example No. 49

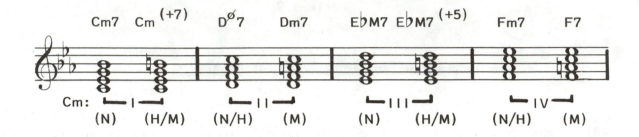

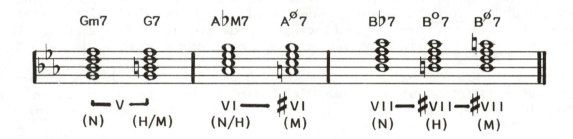

In the following **modal** scheme, study each seventh chord presented. Again, attempt to associate the chordal qualities with their respective Roman numeral designations. This is a difficult area of study and a valuable asset to possess. When working with modal harmony, it is important to understand that only four basic modes are utilized: the **Dorian**, the **Phrygian**, the **Mixolydian**, and the **Aeolian**. Since the Ionian mode and the major scale form are identical, the Ionian is presented only as a guide for the comparison of chordal qualities.

Example No. 50

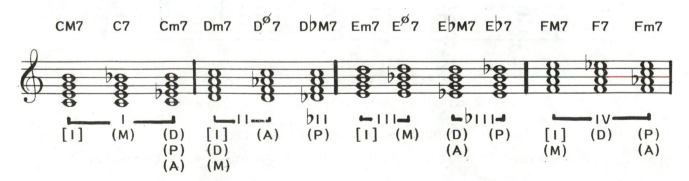

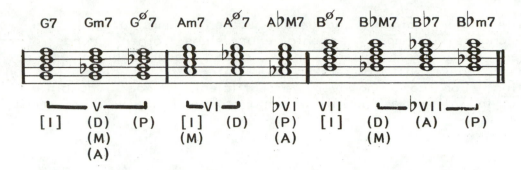

The following reference chart further organizes each chordal scale degree as it pertains to the **major**, **minor**, and **modal** scale schemes.

CHORDAL
DERIVATION
IDENTIFICATION
&
ROMAN NUMERAL DESIGNATION

CHORDAL QUALITY	MAJOR SCALE SCHEME	MINOR SCALE SCHEME	MODAL SCALE SCHEME
Major Seventh Chord	I7; IV7	IlI7; IlI7$^{(+5)}$; VI7 (N) (H/M) (N/H)	bII7; bIII7; bVI7; bVII7 (P) (D) (P) (D) (A) (A) (M)
Minor/Major Seventh Chord		I7 (H/M)	
Minor Seventh Chord	II7; IlI7; VI7	I7; II7; IV7; V7 (N) (M) (N/H) (N)	I7; IV7; V7; bVII7 (D) (P) (D) (P) (P) (A) (M) (A) (A)
Half–Diminished Seventh Chord	VII7	II7; ♯VI7; ♯VII7 (N/H) (M) (M)	II7; IlI7; V7; VI7 (A) (M) (P) (D)
Dominant Seventh Chord	V7	IV7; V7; VII7 (M) (H/M) (N)	I7; bIII7; IV7; bVII7 (M) (P) (D) (A)
Fully–Diminished Seventh Chord		♯VII7 (H)	

MINOR SCALE ABBREVIATIONS

(N)=Natural   (H)=Harmonic   (M)=Melodic

MODAL SCALE ABBREVIATIONS

(D)=Dorian   (P)=Phrygian   (M)=Mixolydian   (A)=Aeolian

While **major**, **minor**, and **modal** scale schemes provide the majority of working chords in most harmonic expressions, other chords of importance exist, as well. Most often, these chords are categorized as <u>dominant substitutes</u>; they will be taken up later in a discussion on <u>chordal substitution</u>. For now, however, a sufficient chordal vocabulary has been presented to allow a definitive and concise analysis of most harmonic expressions.

<u>SUGGESTED THEORY DRILL</u>

1. In the following harmonic excerpt entitled, **"Have You Met Miss Jones?"** by **Richard Rodgers,** study the analysis given. And then, on your own, select at least ten compositions of your choice and analyse them. Additionally, create your own harmonic expressions, according to what you have learned in **Section 1 & 2,** and analyse them, as well. At this point, sufficient information has been presented to formulate chordal patterns and to understand the beginnings of chordal function.

Section 3

CHORDAL SUBSTITUTION-1

As was previously stated, the theory of **chordal substitution** is based upon the notion of chords sharing common tones. A concept that also states that the greater the number of common tones between chords, the greater the potential is for **chordal substitution**. Intrinsically linked with this idea are the two adjunct concepts of chordal function and tendency. Together, these three elements provide composers, arrangers, and players with a vast reservoir and potential for altering harmonic colors, modifying chordal complexities and achieving desired musical effects.

In the following example the major key scheme has been chosen to illustrate the notion of common tones and to depict, generally, the method for arriving at major, minor, and modal substitutions.

Example No. 51

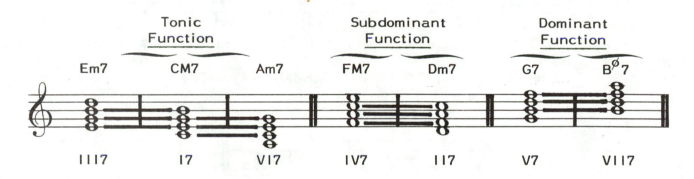

In the above example it is important to note that three seventh chords placed on the mediant [III7], the tonic [I7], and the submediant [VI7] degrees serve the **tonic [I] function**; two additional seventh chords placed on the subdominant [IV7] and supertonic [II7] degrees serve the **subdominant [IV] function**; and the two remaining seventh chords placed on the dominant [V7] and leading tone [VII7] degrees serve the **dominant [V] function**. Occasionally, the submediant [VI7] and the mediant [III7] seventh chords substitute for the **subdominant** and **dominant** areas, respectfully; these substitutions are less successful and more "pastel" in color.

Chords of the ♭II variety are also associated with **chordal substitution**. The <u>roots</u> of these chords are located a **tritone (three whole steps = A4/d5)** above or below the <u>dominant</u> and, for the most part, are considered <u>functional dominants</u>. The first of these chords is traditionally referred to as the **Neopolitan**. It is located on the <u>lowered second degree of a major or minor scale</u> and is most often found in <u>traditional music literature as a triad in first inversion</u> **[N6]**; in contemporary music it is usually found <u>in root position</u> as a <u>major seventh chord</u> -- not unlike the Phrygian II7. It functions as a <u>dominant</u> but, paradoxically, it has all of the qualities of a **I Major Tonality** category. It is important to consider this anomaly when selecting chordal extensions involving this chord.

Although the **Neopolitan [♭II7]** chord is used regularly as a **tritone** substitute, the more commonly found ♭II chords are those which belong to an elite group referred to as "ethnic" or <u>augmented sixth</u> chords. These so-called "ethnic" chords consist of the **Italian** (a three-note chord frequently heard in <u>small</u> groups containing three lead horns); the **German** (the most common four-note chord of the group); and the **French** (also a four-note chord often identified mistakenly as a <u>primary dominant</u> with a <u>flatted fifth</u>).

These specialized chords not only have their <u>roots</u> located a **tritone** away from their related <u>dominants</u> but, also, share the **tonal tritone** of the tonality. It is the **tonal tritone** -- the interval of the **third** and **seventh** degrees of the major or minor scale -- which establishes tonality, generates harmonic movement, and, in this instance, makes **chordal substitution** possible.

<u>Example No. 52</u>

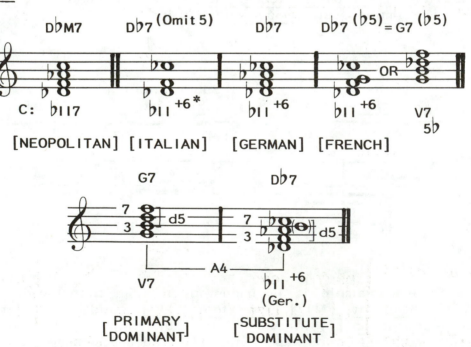

*The **plus six (+6)** placed in the Roman numeral designation is the <u>augmented sixth</u> interval (d♭ to b) used in traditional harmony; however, in <u>the chord</u> symbol as well as in the written chord, the <u>minor seventh interval</u> is chosen to conform to the Alphabetical Chord System.

In addition to forming the basis for **chordal substitution**, tritone sharing yields yet another important concept. By enharmonically respelling a given tritone, alternate root tones provide two possible dominant seventh chords which, in turn, provide two possible chords of resolution. This is all made possible because there can be only six pairs of dominant seventh chords which function as tritone substitutes for each other. The following chart lists each of the six possible pairs of dominant substitutes and, in some cases, their enharmonic equivalents:

1) G7 & Db7(C#7) 2) C7 & Gb7(F#7) 3) Ab7(G#7) & D7

4) Bb7 & E7 5) Eb7 & A7 6) F7 & B7

In the following graphic, study carefully each dual analysis given for the enharmonic respellings of the tonal tritone, the implied alternate bass tones for each pair of dominant seventh chords chosen, and, finally, the two possible chords of resolution.

1) G7
[V7 or bII^{+6}] } CM7 F#M7
or
*Db7 [I7] [I7]
[bII^{+6} or V7]

2) C7
[V7 or bII^{+6}] } FM7 BM7
or
*Gb7 [I7] [I7]
[bII^{+6} or V7]

3) *Ab7
[V7 or bII^{+6}] } DbM7 GM7
or
D7 [I7] [I7]
[bII^{+6} or V7]

4) Bb7
[V7 or bII^{+6}] } EbM7 AM7
or
E7 [I7] [I7]
[bII^{+6} or V7]

5) A7
   [V7 or $\flat II^{+6}$] ⎫
                        ⎬ DM7   A$\flat$M7
   E$\flat$7   ⎭   [I7] or [I7]
   [$\flat II^{+6}$ or V7]

6) B7
   [V7 or $\flat II^{+6}$] ⎫
                        ⎬ EM7   B$\flat$M7
   F7   ⎭   [I7] or [I7]
   [$\flat II^{+6}$ or V7]

*Enharmonic equivalents exist for these chord symbols.

SUGGESTED THEORY DRILL

1. The following harmonic excerpt entitled, **"A Night In Tunisia"** by **Dizzy Gillespie** clearly demonstrates the use of the <u>German</u> and <u>French</u> varieties of the $\flat II+6$ chord.

[PLAY THREE TIMES]   1.

E$\flat$7   Dm   Em7$^{(\flat5)}$ A7$^{(\flat5)}$ Dm

dm: $\flat II^{+6}$ I   II7 $\flat II^{+6}$ I
(GER.)   (FR.)
[V]   [V]

Search for other examples of substitution as it relates to <u>dominant substitutes</u>. It should be understood that <u>tritone substitution</u> occurs most often cadentially as in the compostion entitled, **"A Girl From Ipanema"** by **Antonio Carlos Jobim.**

Gm7   G$\flat$7   FM7

F: II7 $\flat II^{+6}$ I7
    (Meas.5)   [V]   (6)   (7)

2. Create your own harmonic expressions utilizing what you have learned in this **Section.** Be sure to analyze each expression and be able to hear the difference between selected chords of substitution. Also, play some standard compositions and employ what you have learned thus far about **chordal substitution.**

58

Section 4

CHORDAL SUBSTITUTION-II

In the previous section common tones between chords served as a basis for **chordal substitution**. In this section chordal function and tendency will be discussed in more detail.

Chordal function is determined, in large measure, by scale degree location, chordal quality, and influences of the "linear" process. For instance, the strong dominant seventh chord gains its strength from its perfect fifth relationship above the tonic, an interval relationship which is considered to be one of the strongest in all of music. Its chordal quality is unique and different from other chord types; furthermore, it contains the important tonal tritone. Its "linear" pull [Up 4] is most often to the tonic chord, fulfilling its role of establishing tonality. What has been said for the dominant can, in similar fashion, be said for all other chordal degrees found in the major or minor key scheme. Each chordal scale degree has its own particular function and characteristics.

Chordal tendency, on the other hand, is a concept in which chordal roots tend to lean towards other chord roots a half step away. Although intrinsically linked with function, it is the tendency exhibited by the chord which governs its movement. For instance, bII chords, by the nature of their lowered roots, demonstrate a "downward" pull for resolution. So that in a large sense the "linear" process is still a very important consideration.

Chord quality of a singular type, while not absolutely essential, often plays an important role in the concept of tendency. For instance, the **Fully-Diminished Seventh Chord** demonstrates an "up" tendency for chordal resolution, but it should be understood that other chord types demonstrate this tendency, as well.

In summation, the concepts of chordal function and tendency in **chordal substitution** are extremely important to harmonic movement, variation, and the creative process.

To more clearly define **chordal substitution**, study the following material concerning function and tendency of chordal scale degrees in major and minor key schemes. Each chordal scale degree has been identified by its Roman numeral and written name.

MAJOR KEY SCHEME: FUNCTION & TENDENCY

I7 — **Tonic [Major Seventh]** — May progress to any chord in the tonal environment; it is not necessary for establishing tonality, but desirable.

II7 — **Supertonic [Minor Seventh]** — Substitute for the subdominant (IV7) chord; progresses [up 4] to the dominant (V7) chord with great strength; often used in the predominant function (chromatic tendency) to the substitute dominant (♭II7) chord.

III7 — **Mediant [Minor Seventh]** — Substitute for the tonic (I7) chord; progresses [up 4] to the submediant (VI7) with great strength; often heard progressing chromatically through the chromatic (♭III7) chord to the supertonic (II7) chord.

IV7 — **Subdominant [Major Seventh]** — Substitute for the supertonic (II7) chord; progresses with strength [up 2] to the dominant (V7) chord; may progress [dn 3] to the supertonic (II7) chord but not over the bar line and, usually, within the same measure.

V7 — **Dominant [Dominant Seventh]** — Contains the tonal tritone which establishes tonality; progresses [up 4] to the tonic (I7) chord [**Authentic Cadence – See next section**] or may be used in a deceptive manner to any chord other than the tonic (I7) [**Deceptive Cadence – See next section**].

VI7 — **Submediant [Minor Seventh]** — Substitute for the tonic (I7) chord and occasionally for the subdominant (IV7) chord; progresses [up 4] with strength to the supertonic (II7) chord; often heard utilizing its tendency to the chromatic (♭VI7) chord; serves as the tonic (VI7=I7) when modulating to the relative minor.

VII7 — **Leading Tone [Half-Diminished]** — Substitute for the dominant (V7) chord; progresses [up 2] with good strength to the tonic (I7) chord; may progress [dn 3] to the dominant (V7) chord within a measure but seldom over a bar line.

MINOR KEY SCHEME: FUNCTION & TENDENCY

I7 — **Tonic [Minor Seventh] (N)** — May be used in the beginning or within the body of a composition, seldom heard as the final chord; may progress to any chord in the tonal environment.

Tonic [Minor/Major] (H/M) — May be used throughout the composition but has a 50% distortion factor which tends to make it harsh; within the proper environment, it may be very effective; may progress to any chord, but care should be given to good voice leading.

60

	Tonic [Minor Add Sixth] (M)	May progress to any chord within the tonal environment; may be used in the beginning, within the body or for the final chord of the composition.
II7	Supertonic [Half-Diminished] (N/H)	Substitution for the subdominant (IV7–N/H); progresses [up 4] to the dominant (V7–N/H/M) chord with great strength; often heard progressing through its tendency to the substitute dominant (♭II7 & ♭II+6) chord.
	Supertonic [Minor Seventh] (M)	Substitution for the subdominant (IV7–M) chord; heard as a borrowed II7 chord from the parallel major; progresses [up 4] to the dominant (V7–H/M) chord with great strength; often used in the predominant function (chromatic tendency) to the substitute dominant (♭II7) chord.
III7	Mediant [Major Seventh] (N)	Functions as the relative tonal center (I7–N) for the relative major; substitute for the tonic (I7–N) chord; works well [up 4] to the submediant (IV7–N/H) and enjoys considerable use utilizing its tendency to the supertonic (II7–N/H/M) chord.
	(Raised Fifth–H/M)	Not often used because of its high dissonant factor.
IV7	Subdominant [Minor Seventh] (N/H)	Used as a temporary contrasting tonal center (IV–I7); substitute for the supertonic (II7–N/H) chord; progresses well to the leading tone (VII–N) chord and to the dominant (V7–N/H/M) chord.
	Subdominant [Dominant Seventh] (M)	Most often heard as a secondary dominant (V7 of VII7–N) chord (See next section); has all of the capabilities of its companion subdominant (IV7–N/H) chord.
V7	Dominant [Minor Seventh] (N)	Considered a modal dominant (V7–N) chord with little dominant (V7) strength (lacks the tonal tritone) but effective in the proper surroundings.
	Dominant [Dominant Seventh] (H/M)	Contains the tonal tritone which establishes the tonality; progresses [up 4] to the tonic (I7–N/H/M) chord or may move deceptively to any chord other than the tonic (I7–N/H/M) chord.
VI7	Submediant [Major Seventh] (N/H)	Substitute for the tonic (I7–N/H) chord; occasionally substitutes for the subdominant (IV7–N/H) chord; progresses [dn 2] utilizing its tendency to the dominant (V7–N/H/M) chord and [up 4] to the supertonic (II7–N/H) chord, as well.
♯VI7	Submediant [Half-Diminished] (M)	Most often heard utilizing its tendency and progressing [up 2] to the leading tone (VII–N) chord; progresses [up 4] well to the supertonic (II7–N/H/M) chord; also, utilizing its tendency to the submediant (VI7–N/H) chord and eventually to the dominant

(V7–H/M) chord; may function as a substitute for the tonic (I7–N/H/M) chord and occasionally for the subdominant (IV7–M) chord.

VII7	**Leading Tone** **[Dominant Seventh]** **(N)**	Progresses [up 4] very well to the mediant (III7–N) chord; and works well [up 2] to the tonic (I7–N/H/M) chord.
♯VII7	**Leading Tone** **[Fully–** **Diminished] (H)**	Progresses [up 2] to the tonic (I7–N/H/M) chord; also used as a substitute for the dominant (V7–H/M) chord.
	Leading Tone **[Half–Diminished]** **(M)**	Progresses [up 2] to the tonic (I7–M) chord; also may substitute for the dominant (V7–H/M) chord as a borrowed chord from the parallel major.

SUGGESTED THEORY DRILL

1. Review and evaluate each chord set progression presented in the previous three sections. Attempt to assign a function and/or tendency to each chord set in terms of what you have learned in this section.

2. In addition select at least ten compostions of your choice and follow the same set of directions previously given concerning function and tendency.

3. Notate various progression formulas based upon information presented in this section. In order to further enhance your knowledge, play and hear each of these formulas at the piano.

Section 5

CHORDAL SUBSTITUTION—III

No discussion of **chordal substitution** can be complete without making reference to three additional concepts: **secondary dominants**; **interchangeable chord qualities**; and **dual chord analysis**. They are, collectively, the three remaining techniques to be understood in the study of **chordal substitution**.

Previously, two different types of <u>dominant seventh chords</u> were introduced. By way of review, the first type was labeled as a **primary dominant** and was found on the <u>fifth</u> degree of the "grand key." The so-called "grand key" in that context referred to the <u>tonic</u> (I) degree or keytone of the primary scale or tonality. The second type involved a group of seventh chords which were found on the <u>lowered second degree</u> of a major or minor scale and because they contained in some cases the same "tonal tritone" found in the related **primary dominant** chord were labeled **substitute dominants**.

SECONDARY DOMINANTS

The third and final group to be presented are referred to as **secondary dominants**. Individually, and as a group, they are used to color and strengthen the grand key from which they are derived. Invariably, they contribute the additional means necessary for more involved melodic invention and provide, most often, the harmonic complexity so desirable in a musical expression.

Secondary dominants are located a distance of <u>a perfect fifth</u> above each diatonic and modally altered scale degree of any major or minor scale. The exceptions to this are the obvious <u>tonic</u> (I) degrees -- both major and minor which support **primary dominants** -- and the <u>leading tone</u> (VII) degree of the major scale. The seventh degree provides the <u>root tone</u> for a diminished triad and, as such, cannot support or tolerate within the tonality of the grand key a **secondary dominant**. In other words scale degrees in their natural or altered state which provide root tones for major or minor triads can and do support **primary** as well as **secondary dominants**. Scale degrees which provide root tones for augmented and diminished triads, with the exception of the <u>supertonic</u> (II) degree in minor, do not. Thus, in the grand key scheme of C major, the **primary dominant** of the <u>tonic</u> (I) degree is a **G7** chord; the **secondary dominant** of the <u>supertonic</u> (II) degree is an **A7** chord; above the <u>mediant</u> (III) degree, the **secondary dominant** would be a **B7** chord; and, in similar fashion, above the <u>subdominant</u> (IV) degree a **C7** chord, above the dominant (**V**) degree, a **D7** chord; and, finally, above the <u>submediant</u> (**VI**) degree, an **E7** chord. The <u>leading tone</u> (**VII**) degree in major, as was previously stated, does <u>not</u> support a **secondary dominant**. **Secondary dominants**, in general, enjoy all of the capabilities and potential of **primary dominants** and function in much the same manner as well.

When formulating an analysis of a given harmonic expression in which **secondary dominants** are employed, it is important to show the analysis in the following manner: **V7** slash **II** (**V/II**) meaning the **secondary dominant** of the <u>supertonic</u> (**II**) chord or in a verbal manner, **V7** of **II**.

The following graphic illustrates the formulation of the **primary** and **secondary dominants** of the grand key of C major.

	Primary Dominant		Secondary Dominants					
C Major	G7	A7	B7	C7	D7	E7		=Seventh Chords
	[V]	V7/II	V7/III	V7/IV	V7/V	V7/VI	N/A	=Analysis
	C	Dm	Em	F	G	Am	Bm (-5)	=Triads
	(I)	(II)	(III)	(IV)	(V)	(VI)	(VII)	=Scale Degrees

INTERCHANGEABLE CHORD QUALITIES

Interchangeable **Chord qualities** simply make reference to chords changing their function and tendency by altering their component parts. To briefly set an example, the <u>mediant</u> (**III7**) chord in C major is normally an **Em7** chord. If, however, its minor triad is changed to major –– among other possibilities –– its function could be that of a <u>dominant seventh chord</u> **E7** and thus, could function as the <u>primary dominant</u> of A major/minor; or as an enharmonic **substitute dominant** ♭**III7(Ger.)** of E♭ major/minor; or as a **secondary dominant V7/II** in the grand key of G major/minor. In as much as there are six varieties of seventh chords, the potential for **interchangeable chord qualities** on all scale degrees in a basic tonality is enormous.

The concept of **interchangeable chord qualities** allows composers, arrangers, and players a wide potential for melodic and harmonic invention. To further pinpoint this potential, examine the possible component changes which could result with just the <u>tonic</u> (**I**) chordal degree of C major. It should be understood that although chordal changeability has taken place in the following instances, many more interpretations of function and tendency exist for each given chordal change.

CM7 = I7 in C Major

<u>**The following additional interpretations are possible.**</u>

$$Cm7 = I7 \text{ in C Minor(N)}$$

or

$$Cm^{(+7)} = I7 \text{ in C Minor(H/M)}$$

or

$$C^{\o}7 = VII7 \text{ in D}\flat \text{ Major}$$

or

$$C7 = \begin{cases} V7/IV \text{ in C Major} \\ \text{or} \\ \flat II7(\text{Ger.}) \text{ in B Major} \\ \text{or} \\ V7 \text{ in F Major} \end{cases}$$

or

$$C^{o}7 = VII7 \text{ in C}\sharp(\text{D}\flat) \text{ Minor(H)}$$

Related to the concept of **interchangeable chord qualities** is the subject of **dual analysis**. It can best be described as the act of **(1)** selecting a <u>pivot chord</u> which is <u>common</u> to two tonalities; **(2)** interpreting the function and tendency of the <u>pivot chord</u> within the two tonalities; and **(3)** labeling the <u>pivot chord</u> separately for the purposes of analysis. The process described is identical to the act of diagramming <u>pivotal modulation</u>. Aurally, the process allows the composer/arranger the necessary flexibility to write temporary and permanent tonal shifts which are subtle and smooth rather than abrupt and sudden.

Selecting a <u>common pivot chord</u> is best achieved by selecting a seventh chord which sounds diatonically the same in two tonalities. The chord may or may not be spelled the same; in many instances enharmonically equivalent chord spellings qualify as <u>pivot chords</u>.

The following example more clearly defines the process of **dual analysis**; study it carefully.

An **Em7** chord could be interpreted as a <u>mediant</u> (III7) chord in the key of C major and could also be interpreted as a <u>submediant</u> (VI7) chord in the key of G major. Since the **Em7** contains the same pitch components in both keys, it can serve as the <u>pivot chord</u> for **dual analysis**. The <u>pivot chord</u>, in this instance, serves as the bridge or transitional chord between the two tonalities chosen. Or, in other words, the <u>pivot chord</u> is a chord which is arrived at in one key and left in another and thereby provides the exit and entry from one tonal center to another. The act of <u>modulation</u> is fulfilled when the <u>pivot chord</u> in the new key is led logically through melodic materials with sufficient duration of time to a two or three chord cadence comprised of <u>subdominant</u> and <u>dominant</u> quality chords.

To more clearly understand the process, study, play, and hear the following harmonic expressions. Also, it should be understood that perpendicular lines make reference to measures, while slanted lines represent the beat.

Example No. 53a

Example No. 53b

Example No. 53c

66

SUGGESTED THEORY DRILL

1. In a standard "fakebook" search through at least ten compositions investigating the many uses of **secondary dominants**. Two excellent sources for additional investigation would be the **"Chorales"** of **Johann Sebastian Bach** and the **"Mazurkas"** of **Frederic Chopin**. Be sure not to confuse **primary** with **secondary dominants**. Consult the chapter as often as needed.

2. After having searched for **secondary dominants**, return to the same sources and search for uses of **interchangeable chord qualities**. They are most often found as <u>pivot chords</u> in connection with the concept of **dual analysis**.

3. Create ten harmonic phrases of four bars in length. In the first five examples utilize two chord symbols per measure. In the second group of five measures utilize four chord symbols per measure. Each of these should be placed in quadruple time and performed at the piano. If you don't play the piano, it might be wise to have someone who does record each example from this chapter as well as your phrases for ear training purposes.

4. Continue to pursue an investigation of all of the material discussed in this chapter. Popular music has made extensive use of these concepts, and it is important to thoroughly understand them.

Section 6

HARMONIC PULSE

The success or effectiveness of a chord progression is largely determined by the position it occupies within the given parameters of measured time. If a progression is grammatically correct but poorly placed within a measure or a multiple measure grouping, the progression will sound incorrect. It is, therefore, imperative that **harmonic pulse** be studied along with chordal formulas to help insure the most effective means for creative harmonic expression.

In the study of rhythm measured time makes reference to relationship of strength and weakness among beats in simple or compound measures of music. A thorough knowledge of how individual beats relate to **harmonic pulse** through this rhythmic stress is absolutely essential. Rhythmically speaking, all time signatures demonstrate this involvement of stress planes within a measure as well as in multiple measure groupings. The following sets of time signatures are presented for clarification. Also, the single tick mark (') indicates a slightly less strong pulse while the double ('') and triple (''') tick marks indicate progressively weaker pulse beats or fractions of beats.

SIMPLE & COMPOUND TIME SIGNATURES

Category	Sample Time Signatures	Example:

Simple
Duple
Time
$\frac{2}{16}$ $\frac{2}{8}$ $\frac{2}{4}$ $\frac{2}{2}$

S w S w S w S w

Etc.

Simple
Triple
Time
$\frac{3}{16}$ $\frac{3}{8}$ $\frac{3}{4}$ $\frac{3}{2}$

S w w' S w w' S w w'

Etc.

69

Simple **Quadruple** Time	4 8	4 4 (or C)	4 2

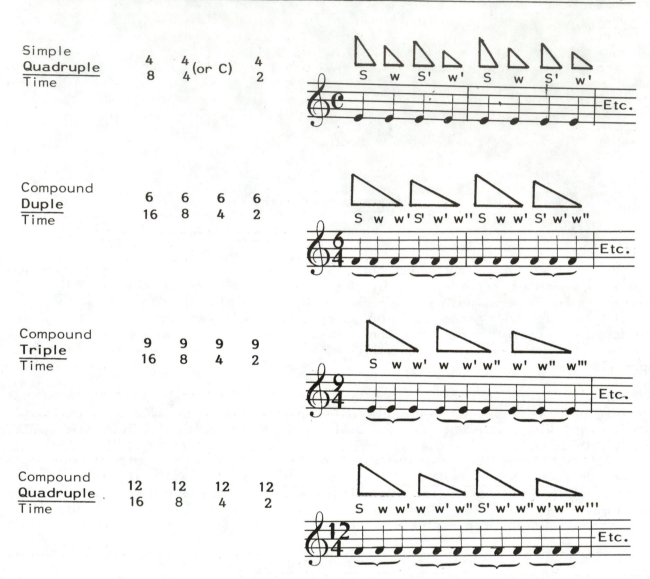

Compound **Duple** Time	6 16	6 8	6 4	6 2

Compound **Triple** Time	9 16	9 8	9 4	9 2

Compound **Quadruple** Time	12 16	12 8	12 4	12 2

Two Examples of Asymmetrical Time Signatures

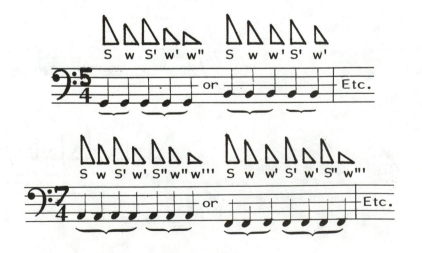

Previously, a reference was made concerning the "involvement of stress planes within multiple measure groupings." This notion states that <u>measured time</u> tends to arrange itself in multiples of two; that is to say, the first measure of any two measure phrase will be strong while the subsequent measure will be weak. Similarly, if a phrase is four measures or more in length, the first two measures will be stong and the third and fourth measures weak and so forth. With few exceptions <u>measured music</u> tends to arrange itself in this manner, no matter what the time signature. The following illustrations should clarify this notion.

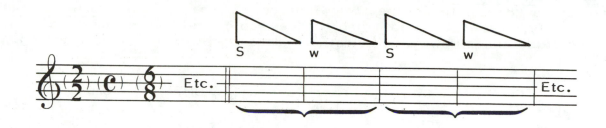

Similarly:

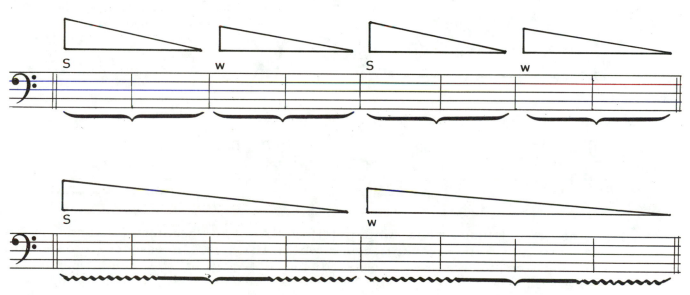

When subdividing an individual beat within a measure, the plane of stress is, again, from stong to weak.

The proper matching of **harmonic** and **rhythmic** components serves as the guiding principle for the writing of effective and successful harmonic progressions. Generally, chords of the **dominant** persuasion are used to activate weak beats within a measure or weak measures within a multiple measure grouping. This method of activating weak segments of a musical notion allows for a natural forward motion to take place. Although **dominants** are found on strong beats within a measure or in multiple measure groupings, their sound, more often than not, is usually extended through the weaker portions of the musical expression; moreover, final cadences or endings often utilize the placement of **dominant** chords on beats or measures which cause a loss of forward motion. While this device is not effective in the beginning or body of a composition, the "slowing down" or loss of forward motion, harmonically, could be and often is desirable and quite acceptable in an ending. Study the following illustrations for a more precise understanding.

F6 / / C7 / / (4/4) S' (———→)	DM7 / / Gm7 A7 (4/4) w' (———)
A7 / / Ab7 / / (C) S w S' w' (———————→)(———————→)	Eø7 / / A7(b9) (¢) S w (———————→)
FM7 / / Db7 / (3/4) w' (———→)	Dm7 / / G7 / / (3/4) w (———————→)

Of the two illustrations which follow **(A)** has greater forward motion with more activity in the weak measure while **(B)** has, in essence, created an imaginary bar-line to the left, lessened the activity in the weak measure of the multiple measure grouping, and created a "slowing down effect" which may be acceptable in an ending musical expresssion.

(A) (4/4) GM7 / / / | Cm7 / / D7(b9) / / | G6 /
S   w   (S')   S
                                  (————————————→)

(B) (4/4) GM7 / / | Cm7 / / | D7(b9) / / / | G6 /
S   (S')   w   S
                                   (————————————————→)

Finally, the endings of rhythmic divisions are characterized by what are referred to as cadences. These cadences are analogous to punctuation in written English. Although they are most often thought of as rhythmic concepts, they are largely governed by **harmonic pulse** and associated with certain harmonic patterns. The following categories of cadences are presented for study.

CADENCES

1. "AUTHENTIC" CADENCE:

The use of this cadence is characterized by a feeling of finality and is used in the same manner as one would use a period in written English. The harmonic pattern associated with this cadence is the **dominant** to **tonic (V to I)** progression. This cadence contains the tonal tritone and, as such, is the strongest cadence available.

2. "PLAGAL" CADENCE:

The plagal cadence **(IV to I)** is often referred to as the **"Amen"** cadence because of its historical and constant use in church music. It contains a certain degree of finality, but it is considerably less energetic and more passive than the **authentic** cadence. Its root movement is up a fourth and classified as "secondary." Also, it contains no tonal tritone.

3. "DECEPTIVE" CADENCE:

This cadence is characterized by its **deceptive** nature. Although containing the **dominant** chord with the strength of the tonal tritone, this cadence does not carry out its expected intention and for that reason is descriptively referred to as **deceptive**. Its use in musical composition is extension, and its purpose is prolongation. Any chord other than the **tonic** when progressing from the **dominant** in a cadence of this nature would be considered **deceptive (V to any chord other than I).**

4. "HALF" CADENCE:

The **half** cadence **(V)** is perhaps the hardest to describe. It is usually found at the end of a rhythmic division and contains a chord of tendency; moreover, this chord of tendency is most often a **dominant** quality chord. Perhaps, the clearest example of a **half** cadence can be found at the end of any **"1st ending"** or **"turn around"** in a musical composition.

SUGGESTED THEORY DRILL

1. Return to each of the compositions you have examined up to now and make a detailed analysis of those items related to **harmonic pulse**. Be sure to investigate the following: the time signature and its classification; the involvement of stress planes in each rhythmic division; the matching of harmonic and rhythmic components; the placement and use of **dominant** harmony in each individual measure and in multiple measure groupings; and the use of cadences.

2. After you have made a thorough investigation of the principles of **harmonic pulse**, attempt to write several original measures of music yourself. Be sure to utilize all of what you have learned in this section of the text. Play each musical expression at the piano and listen critically to what you have written.

[NOTES]

Section **7**

HARMONIC FORMULAS-I

The ability to successfully write and create effective **harmonic formulas** is predicated on a knowledge of **(1)** chords and their function; **(2)** root movement; **(3)** chordal substitution; and **(4)** harmonic pulse. The reference to chordal function in the first instance involves the assignment and placement of various chord types to tonal areas within the harmonic scheme, a scheme which most often involves the **pre-dominant, dominant,** and **tonic tonal areas** of a given tonality. These tonal areas will be explored in greater detail in the following pages. Root movement, chordal substitution, and harmonic pulse have already been presented and should be referred to whenever the need arises to clarify and strengthen the new material presented.

THE SUBDOMINANT-DOMINANT-TONIC PROGRESSION

The most commonly used **harmonic formula** in traditional harmony is the subdominant to dominant to tonic progression with all of its many variants. More often referred to as the **IV-V-I** progression, its regularity of use is prominent in all music. Its strength is based upon strong root movement and clear linear motion. Although heard extensively in contemporary commercial music, the **pre-dominant** area of the subdominant is replaced with its diatonic variant (substitute supertonic (II7) chord) in jazz and is often referred to as the **II-V-I** progression.

Diatonic Variants

$$\begin{array}{llll} \text{4} & \text{FM7} & \text{G7} & \text{CM7} \\ \text{4} & / \ / \ / \ / & |/ \ / \ / \ / & \| \\ & \text{(IV)} & \text{(V)} & \text{(I)} \end{array} \qquad \begin{array}{llll} \text{4} & \text{Dm7} & \text{G7} & \text{CM7} \\ \text{4} & / \ / \ / \ / & |/ \ / \ / \ / & \| \\ & \text{(II)} & \text{(V)} & \text{(I)} \end{array}$$

Additional diatonic variants exist through the concept of interchangeability of mode. They are brought about by the immediate interplay and use of major and minor chordal degrees. This creates a certain degree of ambiguity of tonal feeling, but, overall, it helps to create a degree of complexity which is desirable. Study the following possibilities; chord choices are restricted to four and five level chords and placed within the tonalities of **C major** and/or **c minor.** For now, the <u>dominant</u> (V) chord remains the same in either tonality.

<u>Source</u>

	Major		Minor
<u>Tonic</u>	(I) = C6; CM7; C6/9	<u>Tonic</u>	(I) = Cm6; Cm(+7); Cm6/9
			(M) (N/H) (M)
<u>Supertonic</u>	(II) = Dm7	<u>Supertonic</u>	(II) = Dm7(♭5); Dm7
			(N/H) (M)
<u>Subdominant</u>	(IV) = FM7; F6	<u>Subdominant</u>	(IV) = Fm7; Fm6; F7
			(N/H) (N/H) (M)
<u>Dominant</u>	(V) = G7	<u>Dominant</u>	(V) = G7
			(H/M)

Minor Scale Abbreviations
(N) = Natural   (H) = Harmonic   (M) = Melodic

Thus:

The Dominant Tonal Area

By way of <u>chordal substitution</u>, the **dominant tonal area** yields additional chords of the <u>dominant</u> persuasion. These <u>functional dominants</u> can be used individually in place of the <u>primary dominant</u> without creating any problems of tonal instability. This specifically means that they can be exchanged freely when using interchangeable modes of major and minor of the same letter name. The first of these chords is referred to as a diatonic substitute and is found, more often than not, as a **Fully-Diminished Seventh chord** located on the seventh degree (VII) of the major/minor scale. This chord tends to create a "pastel" shading of sorts and, as a result, is not used very often. The group of chords most often used as dominant substitutes, however, are chords of the ♭II variety. All of these chordal substitutes, including the **Fully-Diminished Seventh Chord**, contain, with one notable exception, the same tonal tritone found in the primary dominant.

It should be understood at this point that chordal substitution is based upon several considerations, one of which is melody. While it is not the intent or purpose of this text to discuss melodic invention, it is important to state that all **harmonic formulas** are affected by melodic treatment and voicings.

Source

Major		Minor	
Dominant	= G7 (V)	Dominant	= G7 (V)
Leading Tone	= Bm7(♭5) (VII)	Leading Tone	= B°7; Bm7(♭5) (VII–H) (VII–M)
Substitute Dom.	= D♭7; D♭M7 (♭II) (♭II–Neop.)	Substitute Dom.	= D♭7; D♭M7 (♭II) (♭II–Neop.)

The Neopolitan chord does not contain the tonal tritone.

Thus:

and even:

The examples shown on the previous page were presented as an indication of some of the posssible combinations most frequently encountered; bear in mind that there are numerous other combinations which have not been presented. (See **Book V** (addendum) for additional **harmonic formulas**.)

SUGGESTED THEORY DRILL

Before doing this assignment, read the entire series of statements carefully; some parts of this assignment are interrelated.

1. Select new compositions from your "fake" book and search for **harmonic formulas** discussed in this section. Keep in mind these formulas can appear in the beginning, middle, or ending of a musical composition; and, of course, they may appear in cadences.

2. Lift out of context each formula selected and analyze each aspect of its personality. Bracket and identify **pre-dominant**, **dominant**, and **tonic** tonal areas; indicate Roman numerals along with minor scale designations; investigate chordal placement within the **harmonic pulse** of each measure; scrutinize each chordal substitution for function; observe **root movement** between chords; and, finally, begin writing these formulas down in a small notebook for easy reference and practice.

3. Spend some time relating the melodic structure of each formula to specific chordal choices. Does the melody utilize chord tones or passing tones and, if so, which degrees do these notes represent with the chordal alignment and chord scale? As you relate and compare, look for common degree choices which tend to appear over and over again. After you have completed this drill to your satisfaction, write some original **harmonic formulas** keeping in mind all of what you've learned so far. In addition add melodic interest to your formulas. Be sure to utilize all of the information you have gathered in your investigation of melodies as well.

4. Additional sources of music for the above activities can be obtained from popular sheet music, songbooks, piano books, guitar books, Bach Chorales, and various other sources too numerous to mention.

Section 8

HARMONIC FORMULAS-II

In the previous section on **harmonic formulas** the most common progression in traditional harmony was introduced involving the **pre-dominant, dominant,** and **tonic** tonal areas. Diatonic variants of this very important progression were also introduced through the interchangeability of mode and chordal substitution concepts. In addition the **dominant** tonal area was explored and given more dimension. In this section a broader perspective of possible chord substitutes will be investigated for chords of the **pre-dominant** tonal area.

The Pre-Dominant Tonal Area

Chords of the **pre-dominant tonal area** which lead directly and persuasively to the dominant fall into two main categories: chords which are related to the primary dominant (**V**) and those of the substitute dominant (♭**II**). These primary and substitute dominants, which are placed within the **dominant tonal area,** serve as the basis upon which chords of the **pre-dominant tonal area** are derived and ultimately selected. To better understand this statement of importance, consider these functional dominants as chords which are functioning as temporary tonics in need of a chord or series of chords to be placed directly in front of them. From this point of view, the selection of chords for the **pre-dominant tonal area** becomes relatively easy to calculate and derive. As in the previous section, all diagrams and examples are placed in the tonalities of either **C major** and/or **c minor;** moreover, they may be presented with chordal extensions and/or alterations according to chord types.

Source

Secondary Dominants	(--→)	Functional Dominants
		(Primary)
D7		G7
(~~V/V~~ or V)		(~~V~~ or I)
		(Substitute)
A♭7		D♭7
(~~V/♭II~~ or V)		(~~♭II~~ or I)
		(Substitute)
A♭7		D♭M7
(~~V/♭II Neop.~~ or V)		(~~♭II Neop.~~ or I)

Thus:

$\begin{array}{l}
\text{4} \quad \text{D7(b9)} \quad \text{G7} \quad \text{Db7} \quad \text{C6/9} \\
\text{4} \quad / \ / \quad / \ / \quad |/ \ / \quad / \ / \quad \| \\
\text{(V/V)}
\end{array}$
$\qquad$
$\begin{array}{l}
\text{4} \quad \text{Ab7(5)} \quad \text{Db7} \quad \text{Cm6/9} \\
\text{4} \quad / \ / \quad / \ / \quad |/ \ / \quad / \ / \quad \| \\
\text{(V/bII)}
\end{array}$

$\begin{array}{l}
\text{4} \quad \text{Ab9} \quad \text{Db6/9} \quad \text{CM9} \\
\text{4} \quad / \ / \quad / \ / \quad |/ \ / \quad / \ / \quad \| \\
\text{(V/bII-Neop.)}
\end{array}$
$\qquad$
$\begin{array}{l}
\text{4} \quad \text{D7(b5)} \quad \text{G7} \quad \text{Db9} \quad \text{CM9} \\
\text{4} \quad / \ / \quad / \ / \quad |/ \ / \quad / \ / \quad \| \\
\text{(V/V)}
\end{array}$

and even:

$\begin{array}{l}
\text{4} \quad \text{Ab9} \quad \text{G7} \quad \text{C6/9} \\
\text{4} \quad / \ / \quad / \ / \quad |/ \ / \quad / \ / \quad \| \\
\text{(bII/V)}
\end{array}$
$\qquad$
$\begin{array}{l}
\text{4} \quad \text{Ab9} \quad \text{G7} \quad \text{Db9} \quad \text{Cm6/9} \\
\text{4} \quad / \ / \quad / \ / \quad |/ \ / \quad / \ / \quad \| \\
\text{(bII/V)}
\end{array}$

Additionally, all interrelated **dominants** can be preceded by their interchangeable supertonic (II) chords. For example, the primary dominant (G7), the two substitute dominants (Db7 & DbM7), as well as the two secondary dominant chords (D7 & Ab7) may interchangeably utilize the following supertonic (II) seventh chords: Dm7, Dø7; Am7, Aø7; Ebm7, Ebø7; Abm7 and Abø7. The supertonic chords (Abm7 & Abø7) are related to the two substitute dominant chords (Db7 & DbM7) by way of a tritone relationship and, as such, will be referred to analytically in this text as (II-TT/R) and (II-N/H-TT/R). Study each type of dominant presented and its relationships in the expanded source diagram below.

Source

Secondary Dominants	(-->)	Functional Dominants

		(Primary)
Am7		Dm7
(II)	D7	(II)	G7
Aø7	(V/V or V)	Dø7	(V or I)
(II-N/H)		(II-N/H)

		(Substitute)
Ebm7		Abm7
(II)	Ab7	(II-TT/R)	Db7
Ebø7	(V/bII or V)	Abø7	(bII or I)
(II-N/H)		(II-N/H-TT/R)

		(Substitute)
Ebm7		Abm7
(II)	Ab7	(II-TT/R)	DbM7
Ebø7	(V/bII-Neop. or V)	Abø7	(bII Neop. or I)
(II-N/H)		(II-N/H-TT/R)

Thus:

$\frac{4}{4}$ Am7   D7 G7   C6/9 / / / / |/ / / / ‖
(II)   (V)

$\frac{4}{4}$ A^ø7   D7 G7(♭9) Cm6 / / / / |/ / / / ‖
(II)   (V)
N/H)

$\frac{4}{4}$ E♭m7 A♭7 G7 CM7 / / / / |/ / / / ‖
(II)   (V)

$\frac{4}{4}$ E♭^ø7 A♭7 D♭7 C6/9 / / / / |/ / / / ‖
(II− (V)
N/H)

$\frac{4}{4}$ E♭m7 A♭9 D♭9 CM9 / / / / |/ / / / ‖
(II)   (V)

$\frac{4}{4}$ E♭^ø7 A♭7 D♭M7 C6 / / / / |/ / / / ‖
(II− (V)
N/H)

and even:

$\frac{4}{4}$ E♭m7 D7 G7   C6/9 / / / / |/ / / / ‖
(II/♭II)

$\frac{4}{4}$ Am7 A♭7 D♭M7 CM9 / / / / |/ / / / ‖
(II/V)

$\frac{4}{4}$ A^ø7   A♭7 G7 Cm6/9 / / / / |/ / / / ‖
(II/V) (♭II/V)

$\frac{4}{4}$ E♭^ø7 D7 G7(♭9) Cm6 / / / / |/ / / / ‖
(II/♭IIm)

$\frac{4}{4}$ Am7 D7 Dm7 G7 CM9 / / / / |/ / / / ‖
(II−V) (II−V)

$\frac{4}{4}$ E♭^ø7A♭7D♭M7D♭7 C6/9 / / / / |/ / / / ‖
(II−V)

$\frac{4}{4}$ E♭m7A♭7A♭m7D♭7 CM7 / / / / |/ / / / ‖
(II−V) (II−V)

$\frac{4}{4}$ E♭^ø7A♭7G7 D♭M7 C6 / / / / |/ / / / ‖
(II−N/H−♭II/V)

    The following composite source diagram illustrates all of what has been presented so far concerning the **pre-dominant**, **dominant**, and **tonic** tonal **areas**. In the process of studying this material every attempt should be made to grasp the method by which these chordal choices and combinations have been selected.

Pre-Dominant	(--->)	Dominant	(--->)	Tonic

Dm7;   Dm7(♭5);
(II&II–M)   (II–N/H)
FM7; Fm7;   F7;
(IV) (IV–N/H) (IV–M)
F6; Fm6;
(IV) (IV–N/H)   G7;
D7;   (V)   C6; CM7; C6/9;
(V/V)   Bm7(♭5);   B°7;   (I)   (I)   (I)
Am7;   A⌀7;   (VII&VII–M) (VII–H)   Cm6; Cm(+7); Cm6/9;
(II/V)   (II–N/H/V)   D♭7;   D♭M7;   (I–M) (I–H/M)   (I–M)
A♭7;   (♭II)   (♭II–Neop.)
(V/♭II&♭II–Neop.&♭II/V)
E♭m7;   E♭⌀7;
(II/♭II) (II–N/H/♭II)
A♭m7;   A♭⌀7;
(II–TT/R) (II–N/H–TT/R)

Although the following chords flagged with an asterick (*) are being presented as parts of related tonal areas to the **dominant**, they may also be interpreted as functioning diatonic chordal degrees within the grand keys of **C major** and/or **c minor**. More context and more consideration to other variables are needed to make an informed decision as to the implied tonality of a musical expression; however, <u>dual analyzes</u> does exist harmonically and the cases presented in this context <u>help</u> illustrate this point. Additionally, it should be understood that the **harmonic formulas** presented represent a small fraction of what is musically possible. (See **Book V** (addendum) for additional **harmonic formulas**.)

Thus:

FM9   Dm9*G9   CM7
(IV)

Am7   D7 D♭7   C6
(II/V)

A♭7   G7(♭9)   Cm6/9
(♭II/V)

E♭m7   Dm7 D♭7   C6/9
(II/♭II)   (♭II)

Am7*   B°7 G7   CM7
(II/V)

D7   Dm7 G7   C6
(V/V) (II–V)

Am7*   A♭7 D♭M7 C6/9
(II/V)

Fm7 B°7 G7   D♭M7 Cm6/9
(IV–N/H)

SUGGESTED THEORY DRILL

1. Re-harmonize a number of selected **harmonic formulas** involving changes to the **pre-dominant** and **dominant tonal areas.** Play these substitutions at the piano utilizing the harmonic content only. Try several choices in each tonal area.

2. Take these same **harmonic formulas** and analyze the melodic content. For example, against a <u>dominant</u> **G7** chord, an original melody consisting of four eighth notes (a♭, g, f, & e) and a half note (d) represent in terms of a **G7** chord the ♭**9th, root, 7th,** and **5th** degrees, respectively. If a **Dm7** chord is chosen to replace the <u>dominant</u> **G7** chord for four of the first five tones of the measure, the chord tones would represent the following degrees of the **Dm7** chord: the ♭**5th, 11th, 3rd,** and **9th,** respectively. All of these tones are acceptable chordal and altered degrees of the **Dm7** chord. What this important statement means is that if the melodic degrees being considered are acceptable chordal and altered degrees of the <u>substitute</u> chord, the change of <u>substitution</u>, melodically, will be successful and, most often, effective.

3. As in the previous theory drill, write down your most successful substitutions so as to create a musical diary for reference, review, and practice. Continue to do as many of these **harmonic formulas** as possible. Your constant practice and use of the these important principles of composition will repay you many times over in your pursuit of musical excellence.

[NOTES]

Section 9

In the previous two sections of this text new methods for expanding and selecting chordal substitutes for the **pre-dominant** and **dominant tonal areas** were presented. In addition special consideration was given to sources of interrelated tonal areas. For example, interchangeability of mode offered the unexpected interaction of the parallel major and minor tonalities while substitute and secondary dominants paved the way for the blending of distant tonalities. In this section the importance of the **tonic tonal area** will be explored.

The Tonic Tonal Area

All musical expressions are affected by chordal choices of the **tonic tonal area**. Degrees of strength, vitality, and direction are all shaped by considerations pertaining to this most important locale. Tonic area chords, which directly follow those of the **dominant tonal area**, may function as truly tonic choices or form the basis for a temporary involvement of other tonalities. This shifting of tonal centers may affect the direction and/or stability of the tonalities involved.

Although there are many successful possibilities for chordal selection, there remains within the literature certain functional tonic substitutions which have been in constant use and still remain mainstay options for many composers. The following source diagram presents these widely used substitutes involving the **tonic tonal area**.

Primary Dominants   (⟶)   Functional Tonic Substitutes

Em7
(III or II or I)

G7   C
(V)   Major

Am7
(VI or II or I)

- -

E♭M7   E♭6   E♭6/9
(III-N or I)   (III-N or I)   (III-N or I)

E♭M7(+5)
(III-N/M or I)

G7(♭9)   c
(V)   Minor

A♭M7   A♭6   A♭6/9
(VI-N/H or I) (VI-N/H or I) (VI-N or I)

A⌀7
(Dor.VI or II)

As is evident by the source diagram presented, each progression from the appropriate primary dominant seventh chord formulates a deceptive cadence, a cadence whose final chord is a chord other than the true tonic of the intended tonality. In addition each of the substitute chords presented has alternative functions within possible new tonal centers; subsequently, new material will be presented to fully illustrate the manner by which this potential can be utilized.

Perhaps, the most interesting substitution given in the source diagram is the half-diminished seventh chord, placed on the sixth degree in minor. It may function and serve as a Dorian VI chord in minor or as a supertonic (II) seventh chord in a related minor tonality, but, never as an actual substitute tonic chord. Since tonality, by and of itself, can only be sustained through major and minor tonal inferences, diminished chords can not function as true tonics nor can they create tonal centers or tonalities. Therefore, diminished chords never perform the tonic function but are referred to and are part of the functional tonic substitute group.

Finally, until further information is presented, these functional tonic substitutes of the tonic tonal area should be preceded by their primary dominants only. As in previous sections, all harmonic formulas presented have been placed in the tonalities of either C major or c minor and contain chord types with various extensions and/or alterations. Also, detailed information concerning the intended function of a particular chord substitute is presented for clarification and understanding.

Thus:

‖4Dm7   G7   Am7   B⌀7 ‖ / / / / | / / / / ‖‖
(VI, II or I)
Am7 is utilized here as VI and
is followed by the VII chord in
C major.

‖4A♭7   G7   Em7   A7 ‖ / / / / | / / / / ‖‖
(III, II or I)
Em7 is utilized here as II in D
major and is followed by its V7
chord.

‖4D7   G7   A⌀7   Fm7 ‖ / / / / | / / / / ‖‖
(Dor. VI or II)
A⌀7 is utilized here as a Dor. VI
and is followed by Fm7 as IV–N/H
in c minor.

‖4E♭m7 A♭7 G7   A⌀7   D7 A♭7 ‖ / / / / | / / / / ‖‖
(Dor. VI or II)
A⌀7 is utilized here as II–N/H
of g minor and followed by its
V7 & ♭II.

‖4D⌀7   G7(♭9)   E♭M7   A♭M7 ‖ / / / / | / / / / ‖‖
(III–N or I)
E♭M7 is used here as III–N and
is followed by VI–N/H in c minor.

‖4D⌀7   G7sus4   E♭6/9   Cm7 ‖ / / / / | / / / / ‖‖
(III–N or I)
E♭6/9 is used here as I and is
followed by its VI in the new
tonality of E♭ major.

‖4Dm7   G7(♭9)   A♭M7   B♭7 ‖ / / / / | / / / / ‖‖
(VI–N/H or I)
A♭M7 is used as VI–N/H and
followed by the VII–N chord in
c minor.

‖4Dm7   G7(♭9)   E♭M7(+5)   A♭M7 ‖ / / // / | / / / / ‖‖
(III–H/M or I)
E♭M7(+5) is used as III–H/M and
is followed by VI–N/H in c minor.

Now that we have seen what <u>functional tonic substitutes</u> can do in the **tonic tonal area**, let us explore how <u>tonic substitutes</u> can effect change in the **pre-dominant** and **dominant tonal areas**. If the alternative choice of the selected <u>tonic substitute</u> is truly functioning as a new <u>tonic</u> (I) chord, it is possible to engage its <u>primary</u> and/or <u>substitute dominant</u> as well as any qualifying **pre-dominant tonal area** chord. For example, if the new <u>tonic</u> (I) chord is an E♭6/9, it can be immediately preceded by its <u>primary dominant</u> (B♭7) or its enharmonic <u>dominant substitute</u> (E7). And in similar fashion, depending upon which <u>choice</u> of <u>dominant</u> is chosen, any qualifying **pre-dominant tonal area** chord could be placed immediately to the left of the chosen <u>dominant</u> functioning chord to create, temporarily, an entirely new tonal center or tonality.

Thus:

‖4FM7   G7   Em7   Am7 ‖ / / / / | / / / / ‖‖
(IV)   (V)   (III)   (VI)
The Em7 chord is utilized as a III
chord and is followed by a VI chord
in C major.

Could become:

&4/4 F#m7 / / / |/ F7 / / / |/ Em7 / / / |/ Am7 / / / ‖
e: (II)   (♭II)   (I-N)   (IV)

OR

&4/4 F#ø7 / / / |/ B7(♭9) / / / |/ Em7 / / / |/ A7 / / / ‖
e: (II-N/H)(V)   (I-N)
              D: (II)   (V)

The Em7 is used as a temporary tonic with its interchangeable II & substitute dominant (♭II) chords in e minor.

The Em7 is used as a temporary tonic with its own II & V chords while becoming II in D major, instantaneously.

and:

&4/4 Dø7 / / / |/ G7(♭9) / / / |/ A♭M7 / / / ‖
                              (VI-N/H)

The A♭M7 chord in this example is being used as VI-N/H in the tonality of c minor.

Could become:

&4/4 B♭9 / / / |/ E♭7(♭9) / / / |/ A♭M7 / / / ‖
(V/V)   (V)   (I)

OR

&4/4 E♭7(♭5) / / / |/ A7 / / / |/ A♭M7 / / / |/ D♭M7 / / / ‖
(V)   (♭II)   (I)   (IV)

The A♭M7 chord is now used as a temporary tonic in the tonality of A♭ major with its own pre-dominant and dominant chords.

The A♭M7 chord is used here as a temporary tonic in the tonality of A♭ major with its own dominant and substitute dominant chords.

Additional <u>substitute tonic functioning chords</u> exist for the tonalities of **C major** and/or **c minor**. These chords are generally found on the **mediant**, **subdominant**, and <u>altered</u> subdominant degrees. Most often, they serve a double function, serving, on the one hand, as a <u>tonic</u> substitute while simultaneously functioning, on the other hand, as a **pre-dominant** chord. As we have seen in previous examples and will see in examples yet to come, the role of chordal duality or of simultaneous function allows for imaginative tonal flexibility.

<u>Source</u>

Primary Dominants		(——➤)	Functional Tonic Substitutes		
				Eø7 (II-N/H of II)	
G7 (IV)	C Major		F6 (IV)	F6/9 (IV)	FM7 (IV)
				F#ø7 (II-N/H of III)	
- - - - - - - -	- - - - -	- - - - - -	- - - - - -	- - - - - -	- - - - - -
G7(♭9) (V)	c Minor			Fm7 (IV-N/H)	Fm(M7) (I-H/M)

88

Thus:

$\begin{array}{cccc} 4D^{\emptyset}7 & G7(\flat 9) & F\sharp^{\emptyset}7 & B7(\flat 9) \\ 4/ \quad / \quad / \quad / & |/ \quad / \quad / \quad / & | \\ & e:(II-N/H) \; (V) \end{array}$

Could become:

$\begin{array}{cccc} 4Am7 & C\sharp 7 & F\sharp^{\emptyset}7 & F7 \\ 4/ \quad / \quad / \quad / & |/ \quad / \quad / \quad / & | \\ e:(IV-N/H)(V) & (II-N/H)(\flat II) \end{array}$ 　　$\begin{array}{cccc} 4C7(\flat 9) & B7(\flat 9) & GM7 & F\sharp^{\emptyset}7 \\ 4/ \quad / \quad / \quad / & |/ \quad / \quad / \quad / & | \\ e:(V/\flat II) \; (V) & (III) & (II) \end{array}$

and:

$\begin{array}{ccccc} 4D7(\flat 9) & G9(+11) & F6/9 & D\flat M9(+11) & CM9(+11) \\ 4/ \quad / \quad / \quad / & |/ \quad / \quad / \quad / & |/ \quad / \quad / \quad / & | \\ C:(V/V) & (V) & (IV) & (\flat II-Neop.)(I) \end{array}$

Could become:

$\begin{array}{cccccc} 4G9 & G\flat M9 & F6/9 & B\flat M7 & Gm9 & C9(+11) \\ 4/ \quad / \quad / \quad / & |/ \quad / \quad / \quad / & |/ \quad / \quad / \quad / & | \\ F: & (\flat II-Neop.)(I) & (II) & (V) \end{array}$

OR

$\begin{array}{cccccc} 4D\flat 9 & C7(\flat 9) & F6/9 & Dm7 & G9 & C6/9 \\ 4/ \quad / \quad / \quad / & |/ \quad / \quad / \quad / & |/ \quad / \quad / \quad / & | \\ F: & (V) & (I) \\ & C:(IV) & (II) & (V) & (I) \end{array}$

Other examples of <u>functional tonic substitutes</u> can be found in various styles of composition. It should be understood that the **harmonic formulas** presented above represent a small fraction of what is possible when one understands the related concepts of dual analysis or simultaneous function and chordal substitution. The expressions, "dual analysis" and "simultaneous function" are often used interchangeably in chordal analysis. (See Book V (addendum) for additional **harmonic formulas**.)

SUGGESTED THEORY DRILL

1. Re-harmonize a number of selected **harmonic formulas** involving changes to the **pre-dominant, dominant,** and **tonic tonal areas.** Play these formulas at the piano. It is important to digest aurally all of what has been explained thus far. Play each harmonic structure in a vertical manner being sure to sound all of the chordal tones present in the chord symbol.

2. Memorize the formulas presented in the text thus far. As you play or write these formulas, constantly reiterate to yourself the function of the chordal substitute selected and the conceptual mechanism being utilized. It is always important to be able to verbalize about the function and use of the particular device being employed.

3. As in the previous theory drills, write down your most successful **harmonic formulas** in your musical diary for reference, review, and study. Continue to manipulate the various concepts presented so as to create new and stylistic **harmonic formulas** of your own.

4. Finally, select several ballads from a "fakebook" and utilize all of what has been presented thus far concerning the **pre-dominant, dominant,** and **tonic tonal areas.** Attempt to create new and exciting versions of these songs.

[NOTES]

Section 10

HARMONIC FORMULAS–IV

In this final section on "how chords work" we will explore an interesting turnabout concerning the **irregular harmonic substitution** concept, present materials concerning **nonfunctional dominants**, and summarize, in a verbal fashion, everything that has been presented concerning the **three basic tonal areas**.

IRREGULAR HARMONIC SUBSTITUTION

The concept of **irregular harmonic substitution** is primarily concerned with the **tonic tonal area**, a concept involving the coupling of the originally intended tonic chord to the tonality of various **pre-dominant** and **dominant area** substitution chords. For example, in the tonality of **C major** an appropriate tonic tonal substitute could involve the **Em7** chord with its own **pre-dominant** and **dominant tonal area** chords. The turnabout involvement of this progression takes place when the selected **pre-dominant** and **dominant tonal area** chords of the substitute tonality are hooked up with the originally intended tonic, thus formulating an abortive, deceptive, and **irregular harmonic substitution** concerning the **Em7** chord. Although this technique is not widely utilized, it does provide for imaginative harmonic interest and complexity. The essence of what has just been discussed is presented below.

Thus:

$$\text{4Dm7} \quad \text{G7} \quad \text{F\#}^{\phi}\text{7} \quad \text{B7} \quad \text{Em7}$$

C:II   V   (IV–Altered Subdominant)

                          e:II   V   I

The **F#$^{\phi}$7** is acting as a functional tonic substitute (Altered subdominant IV in **C major**) which instantaneously becomes the II–N/H of III (e minor) and is followed by its primary dominant and its regularly expected **Em7** chord.

Could become:

$\begin{array}{llll}\text{4Dm11} & \text{G13(}\flat\text{9)} & \text{F\#}^{\phi}\text{9} & \text{F7(+9) B13(}\flat\text{9) CM13(+11)}\end{array}$

4Dm11 G13(♭9) F#ø9   F7(+9) B13(♭9) CM13(+11)
4/ / / / I/ /   / / I/ / /   / I
C:II   V   (IV—Altered Subdominant)
        e: II   II+6 V   (?)
                    C: I

Again, the F#ø9 is acting as a functional <u>tonic</u> substitute along with the added <u>substitute</u> and <u>primary</u> dominants of e minor. The irregular turnabout substitution occurs when the CM13(+11) -- the originally intended <u>tonic</u> -- is utilized instead of the regularly expected Em7 chord.

Several irregular harmonic substitutions are possible in the parallel tonalities of **C major** and **C minor**. Study the following most commonly heard possibilities and attempt to memorize each unique sound by playing and hearing them several times.

(Key)	(Pre-dom. Area)	(Dom. Area)	(Reg. Tonic)	(Orig. Int. Tonic)
C Major	----------------	B7(V) F7(♭II) FM7(♭II–Neop.)	--- Em7(III)	-------C Maj. or C Min.
C Major	----------------	E7(V) B♭7(♭II) B♭M7(♭II–Neop.)	--- Am7(VI)	------C Maj. or C Min.
C Major	----------------	C7(V) G♭7(♭II) G♭M7(♭II–Neop.)	--- FM7(IV)	------C Maj. or C Min.
— —				
C Minor	----------------	B♭7(V) E7(♭II) EM7(♭II–Neop.)	--- E♭M7(III)	-----C Min. or C Maj.
C Minor	----------------	E♭7(V) A7(♭II) AM7(♭II–Neop.)	--- A♭M7(VI)	----C Min. or C Maj.
C Minor	----------------	C7(V) G♭7(♭II) G♭M7(♭II–Neop.)	--- Fm7(IV)	----C Min. or C Maj.

NONFUNCTIONAL DOMINANTS

Nonfunctional dominants do not function in a conventional way nor do they gain harmonic motion through tonal relationships which serve to stabilize or finalize tonality. Instead, **nonfunctional dominants** work, as in a literary sense, as side plots to the main thread of events in a drama, necessary to the overall existence but not necessarily the fundamental underpinning or superstructure of the main plot. While they are often coupled with their related pre-dominant seventh chords, **nonfunctional dominants** are not always needed in a musical context; however, when they are used, they do provide an unexpected harmonic event which often contributes to the overall outcome of the musical composition. Generally, **nonfunctional dominant seventh chords** do not resolve their dissonant intervals within their own tonal context but, rather, return or lead in an abortive manner to the initial chord of the composition or harmonic phrase. Understanding how **nonfunctional dominants** work does not preclude all of what we have learned in previous sections of this text concerning tonal deceptive functions.

Reviewing how **functional dominants** work may provide a clearer path for the understanding of these **nonfunctional dominants**.

Functional dominants work in the following ways:

1. As part of a root movement scheme in which a primary or substitute dominant seventh chord is followed by a tonic or tonic substitute chord whose root is found **up a perfect fourth** or **down a minor second**;

2. Or, as part of a root movement scheme in which the so-called "Cycle of Fifths" with its two forms is utilized with the related involvement of either of the above root movements;

3. Or, as part of a root movment scheme in which a primary, substitute, or secondary dominant seventh chord is followed by a tonally-related deceptive function. This phase of how **functional dominants** work is often confused with the role and presence of **nonfunctional dominants**.

If the dominant chord in question is not utilized in the above manner, it is said to be a **nonfunctional dominant**. In traditional harmony these **nonfunctional dominants** are more often related to ethnic or augmented sixth chords found on the fourth and flatted sixth degrees of the major scale or fourth and sixth degrees of the minor scale. When doing an analysis of written chord tones, they may be found to be enharmonically misspelled or modified causing an enormous amount of confusion and unwarranted difficulty.

The most prominent **nonfunctional dominant** to be found in today's literature is found on the very first beat of the first measure in traditional blues. This **nonfunctional dominant seventh chord** serves as an indisputable tonic chord and is so designated. Moreover, it may serve a similar role as a **nonfunctional dominant** on the fourth degree in blues and receive the analysis involving the augmented sixth chord group. Note that the attempt to place these dominants in a more traditional analysis is questionable.

Example No. 54

```
   4 C7              F7                C7
  &4/ / / /  |/ / / /  |/ / / / |
   (V/IV=?)          (♭II/III=?)
 C: I7             IV7               I7
                  (IV+6-Ger.)
```

Other examples of this **nonfunctional dominant** can be found again on the fourth degree of a major tonality when it is used between two tonic seventh chords. Note the alternate analysis of the German sixth chord again.

Example No. 55

```
   4 CM7             F7                CM7
  &4/  / / /  |/ / / /  |/ / / / |
                 (V/♭VII=?)
 C: I7             IV7               I7
                  (IV+6-Ger.)
```

Another example of a **nonfunctional dominant** and its use occurs when the flatted sixth degree accompanied by its pre-dominant seventh chord is placed between two tonic seventh chords to create a tonic harmony elaboration. Again, note the flatted sixth chord analysis.

Example No. 56

```
   4 CM7            E♭m7   A♭7      CM7
  &4/  / / /  |/  /  /  /  |/ / / / |
                (II – – V/♭II=?)
 C: I7             ♭VI7              I7
                  (♭VI+6-Ger.)
```

Modal degrees often yield **nonfunctional dominants** in progressions involving the more common flatted third and seventh degrees. These dominant seventh chords form the basis for an interchangeability of mode which adds color and extension to melodic and harmonic invention. As in the previous paragraphs, study carefully each chord function and the suggested analysis.

Example No. 57a

```
   4 C7           E♭7          F7(♭5)        G7
  &4/ / / /  |/  / / /  |/ / / /  |/ / / / |
   (V/IV=?)     (V/♭VI=?)    (V/♭VII=?)
 C: I7          ♭III7        IV7            V7
                            (IV+6-Fr.)
```

94

Example No. 57b

```
  4 C7    /   /   /    B♭7   /   /   /    :‖
  4/  (♭II/VII=?)            (V/♭III=?)
C: I7                    ♭VII7
```

Nonfunctional **dominants** combined with their <u>pre-dominant seventh chords</u> are often seen and heard in chromatically-ascending lines which are headed towards designated **primary**, **substitute**, or **secondary dominant tonal areas**. This compositional device acts as a unifying force in strengthening the overall harmonic scheme and is especially effective in modulatory phrases. The following example illustrates this point.

Example No. 58

```
  4 E♭M7   /   E°7  /    Fm7  /   /   /    B♭7  /   /   /    Gm7  /   /   /    C7  /   /   /  |
  4/       ♯I°7              II7              V7             ⌈III7                  V7
E♭: I7                                                   F: ⌊III7

     A♭m7  /   D♭7  /    Am7  /   /   /    D7   /   /   /    GM7  /   /   /  |
  /          V7              II7              V7              I7
G♭: II7                  G: II7            V7
```

Finally, **nonfunctional dominants** are often <u>seen</u> and <u>heard</u> in <u>serial succession</u>. They are generally coupled with their related <u>pre-dominant seventh chords</u> to form repetitive and fixed patterns of sound without regard for function or traditional tonality. Generally, intervals which equally divide the octave are used; however, any serial succession or combination can be utilized with this compositional device. In each succession the last **nonfunctional dominant** is aimed at a designated **primary**, **secondary**, or **substitute dominant tonal area** to introduce and/or stabilize the intended tonality. The effect of serial succession through repetition of fixed patterns of sound is closely identified with modulatory techniques touched upon in the previous paragraph.

Example No. 59

```
  4 F♯m7 B7   /    E♭m7 A♭7  /    Cm7  F7   /    Am7  D7  A♭7 G6/9  /  |
  4/  /  /  /    /  /  /  /    /  /  /  /    /  /  /  /  /  /  /  /  |
    II7   V7         II7  V7        II7  V7        II7  V7 ♭II+6 I
    └─────┘         └─────┘        └─────┘        └─────┘
       in              in             in             in
    E Major=?       D♭ Major=?     B♭ Major=?      G Major
```

95

SUMMATION OF THE THREE BASIC TONAL AREAS

In conclusion, materials have been presented to show that the **three basic tonal areas** provide the necessary reservoir for harmonic invention, a holding tank -- as it were -- for the countless number of chordal progressions commonly heard and utilized in music composition. The **three** basic areas of concern are the **tonic**, **pre-dominant**, and **dominant tonal areas**.

Of the **three** areas presented and their individual affect on tonality, the **dominant tonal area** tends to occupy the most important position. Within its limits lies the essence and strength for tonality. It is the inclusion of the tonal tritone within the **dominant** complex which provides for this most important element. The tonal area which provides much of the harmonic support and urgency for the **dominant** to appear is the **pre-dominant tonal area**. Its strength is predicated on its dependency for forward motion towards the **dominant**. Of course, some **pre-dominant** chords go directly to the **tonic tonal area**, but it should be remembered that the root movement in the most prominent of cases is secondary (IV to I) and, as such, does not have the forward thrust of a progression containing a primary root movement. Finally, it's the **tonic tonal area** which makes all of what went before it work. It provides for the necessary feeling of repose and finality or the sometimes wanted ambiguity and/or necessary inconclusiveness for extended harmonic invention. In a sense it's the key element which provides for movement to come to a close or to open the door to more extended ideas in a musical composition.

THE FINAL SUGGESTED THEORY DRILL

In this final suggested theory drill every effort should be made to begin a daily regime of study which combines the newly learned concepts of **irregular harmonic substitution** chords and the use of **nonfunctional dominants** with materials previously introduced in earlier sections. To accomplish a thorough understanding of all of these materials, it is essential to write, to analyze, and to hear each exercise you embark upon, daily. In addition weekly analysis of as many compositions as is humanly possible is strongly recommended. Incidentally, the use of a diary concept for filing away analyzed compositions could become a marvelous resource item for quick reference and further study. Finally, by combining one's knowledge of sound theoretical practices, elements of ear-training, and careful analysis of stylistic concerns in the pursuit of harmonic understanding, progress toward musical excellence will be greatly enhanced.

A D D E N D U M

P A R T   V

HARMONIC OVERTONE SERIES

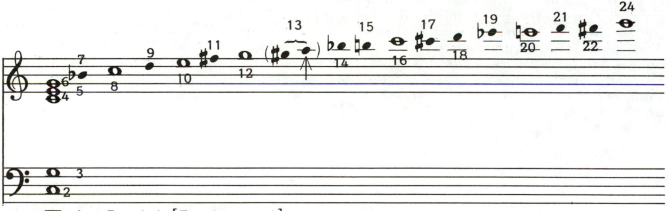

♯ 1st Partial [Fundamental]

Note: In the above example the first six partials with their octave transpositions are represented by whole notes because they are the most audible and the most "in tune" in equal temperament. The thirteenth partial is represented by two blacked-in noteheads with an arrow pointed directly towards the major thirteenth. It is represented in this manner because the thirteenth partial is half-way between the augmented twelfth and the major thirteenth; since the smallest interval of our musical system is the half step or semitone, the major thirteenth is always used.

1. any single pitch, no matter where it is located, is the root tone of an infinite number of harmonic overtones, which gradually diminish in intensity as pitches become higher in sound; therefore, any single pitch is equipped with its own **harmonic overtone series**.

2. Each pitch produces a series of overtones which are referred to as partials. The first partial, which is not considered an overtone, is also referred to as the fundamental. In the above example twenty-four partials are given; however, in chordal alignments and arranged harmony, partials beyond the thirteenth are seldom, if ever, used.

3. The mathematical system of describing pitch in the **harmonic overtone series** is largely identified with controlling the speed of vibration as it affects musical sounds. Highness or lowness of a musical pitch, whether it is produced by strings (string instruments, to include piano, guitar, etc.) or instruments utilizing a wind column such as woodwinds and brass instruments, are generally controlled by the adjustments to the speed of the vibrating body. Thus, with musical instruments the length of a string or wind column coupled with the intensity of the vibration will produce the highness or lowness of a pitch. The shorter the string or column, the higher the pitch and vice versa.

4. The second, fourth, octave, and sixteenth partials are octave transpositions of the fundamental or first partial. They, in fact, represent a doubling of vibration frequencies and as such are extremely easy to compute. For example, all twelfth and sixth partials are octave doublings of the related third partial. In a contrasting method for computing these octave doublings, the fifth partial is represented by octave doublings at the tenth and twentieth partials.

5. Through mathematical computations and/or ratios, intervals of pitch are produced. For example, the 2:1 ratio, according to the **harmonic overtone series** presented, produces a perfect octave. That is to say, that any second partial above a related first partial in any **harmonic overtone series** will produce a perfect octave. In a similar manner the ratio of 6:5 produces an interval of a minor third, a ratio of 7:4 produces a minor seventh, and so forth and so on.

6. Examine carefully the following table of intervallic relationships as they relate to the order and strength of each vibration frequency ratio.

INTERVALLIC RELATIONSHIPS

Interval Strength Categories	Intervals in order of Harmonic Strength	Vibration Frequency Ratios
Strong	1. Perfect Octave	2:1
	2. Perfect 5th	3:2
	3. Perfect 4th	4:3
	4. Major 6th	5:3
	5. Major 3rd	5:4
Medium	6. Minor 7th	7:4
	7. Minor 3rd	6:5
	8. Diminished 5th	7:5
	9. Minor 6th	8:5
Weak	10. Major 2nd	8:7
	11. Major 7th	11.6
	12. Minor 2nd	12:11

Note: The closer the lower number of each ratio or the actual ratio itself is to the first partial the stronger and clearer is the interval. It is said that intervals with low partial numbers are lacking in complexity but, generally, possess greater clarity and strength of sound. In the case of the weak category where the bottom note of the major seventh is lower than the major second, the major second is the stronger interval of the two because it is less complex in structure than the major seventh; its ratio numbers are closer to the first partial.

7. Partials represented in the example by whole notes outline a major triad with octave doublings, indicating that the **harmonic overtone series** in its basic form produces a major triad in sound. All other triads can be represented and accounted for through a system which utilizes the concept of partial distortion. For instance, a minor triad can be represented in the system by flatting (distorting) the fifth partial. When this done, the **harmonic overtone series** in question is said to contain an articulated fifth

partial. All <u>minor</u> <u>triads</u> represent a 33 1/3 <u>distortion</u> level. Incidentally, <u>articulated</u> <u>partials</u> are indicated by a simple checkmark (✓) and are usually placed to the right of the partial number.

Eb HARMONIC OVERTONE SERIES WITH ARTICULATED FIFTH PARTIAL.

8. All chordal alignments, voicings, doublings, and other related areas of discussion in music such as orchestration, arranging, etc., are directly related to the structure of the **harmonic overtone series**. It is imperative that a good grasp of this very important concept be understood and fully utilized.

*　*　*　*　*

THE I-MAJOR TONALITY [I-M]

M13

[P11]--A11

M9

M7

M6

[d5]--P5

P4

M3

ROOT

Note: 1. Although the diminished fifth is given in the above chart, it is seldom employed. When it is used, however, the diminished fifth is usually judged to be the augmented eleventh, expecially when the perfect fifth is included in the alignment.

CHORDAL PLURALITY RELATED TO THE ROOT

Xadd6, XM7, X6/9, XM7sus4

XM9, XM9sus4, X6/9sus4, XM9(+11), X6/9(+11)

XM13(+11)

THE I-MINOR TONALITY [I-m]

M13

P11--[A11]

M9

m7--M7

M6

P5

P4

m3

ROOT

Note: 1. A rule worth repeating in this chord family is that the added sixth is **always** an interval of a **major sixth** above the root of the chord even though it does not agree with what appears in the key signature.

Xmadd6, Xm(+7), Xm6/9, Xm9(+7)

Xm7, Xm9, Xm11

[Xm11(+7)] [Xm13(+7)]

Note: 1. The above chord symbols which are underlined are usually attributed to the II–Major Tonality [II–M] family even though these chords do exist when using the natural form of the minor scale. It is best to think of these as II chords in a major environment [II–M] and not as I–Minor Tonality chords.

2. Chord symbols placed in brackets are possible but are of limited use.

3. Chords utilizing the perfect fourth and the augmented eleventh as "sus" chords are seldom encountered in the minor mode. Usually, these intervals are seen and heard as melodic invention or counter-point and, as such, are not to be considered as part of any specific harmonic alignment.

THE II–MAJOR TONALITY [II–M]

M13

P11

M9

m7

P5

m3

ROOT

Note: 1. The easiest chord family to memorize and the only chord family without interval alterations.

CHORDAL PLURALITY RELATED TO THE ROOT

Xm7, Xm9, Xm11, Xm13

THE II-MINOR TONALITY [II-m]

[~~m13~~]--M13

P11

[~~m9~~]--M9

m7

d5--P5

m3

ROOT

Note: 1. Although the <u>natural</u> minor scale form from which this chord family is derived contains the <u>minor</u> <u>thirteenth</u> and the <u>minor</u> <u>ninth</u>, they are <u>not</u> recommended. As was previously shown in **Part II**, the <u>major</u> <u>thirteenth</u> and the <u>major</u> <u>ninth</u> are borrowed from the <u>parallel</u> <u>major</u>.

2. The alignment utilizing the <u>diminished</u> <u>fifth</u> is by far the most often used **II** chord in the <u>minor</u> tonality.

<u>CHORDAL PLURALITY RELATED TO THE ROOT</u>

Xm7(–5), Xm9(–5), Xm11(–5), Xm13(–5)

<u>Xm7</u>, <u>Xm9</u>, <u>Xm11</u>, <u>Xm13</u>

Note: 1. The above chord symbols which are underlined do exist when using the <u>melodic</u> form of the <u>minor</u> scale and often function as <u>pivot</u> chords for the purposes of <u>modulation</u> between the <u>minor</u> and <u>parallel</u> <u>major</u> tonalities.

THE DOMINANT (MAJOR/MINOR) [V]

[m13]--M13

P11--A11

m9--M9---A9

m7

d5--P5---A5

P4

M3

ROOT

Note: 1. Although the <u>minor</u> <u>thirteenth</u> is heard and seen regularly in popular music, it is most often looked upon as an <u>augmented</u> <u>fifth</u>. It is not found in traditional harmony as a legitimate extension. It is worth noting that the "sus" chordal alignment <u>never</u> includes the <u>third</u>; however, if the <u>third</u> is desired in the alignment, the chord symbol should be changed, voiced, and aligned to show a **dominant ninth** with a **raised eleventh** [X9(+11)].

CHORDAL PLURALITY RELATED TO THE ROOT

1. **Dominant sevenths;**
2. **Dominant sevenths** with **lowered** or **raised fifths;**
3. **Dominant sevenths** with **lowered ninths;**
4. **Dominant sevenths** with **lowered ninths** and **fifths;**
5. **Dominant sevenths** with **raised ninths** and **fifths;**
6. **Dominant sevenths** with **raised ninths** and **lowered fifths;**
7. **Dominant sevenths** with **lowered ninths** and **raised fifths;**

.................and so forth and so on. The **dominant** family structure is the most flexible chordal alignment in all of traditional harmony.

==

THE FULLY-DIMINISHED CHORD GROUPING

Letter Name?

_____

d7

d5

m3

ROOT

Note: 1. Fully-diminished chords are often referred to as "bridging" chords reflecting their most common function in chordal progressions. As was previously shown, these chords are most often used in three and four part alignments. When including one or more notes beyond the <u>diminished</u> <u>seventh</u> <u>interval</u>, it is customary to designate them by their letter names in the chord symbol. <u>Chordal</u> <u>plurality</u> is very limited by virtue of the **equal division** concept. For a more indepth review see **Part III** of this text.

*   *   *   *   *

ADDITIONAL CHORD SETS FOR EAR-TRAINING PURPOSES

CHORD SETS IN FIRST INVERSION*

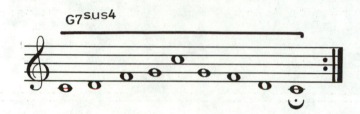

CHORD SETS IN SECOND INVERSION

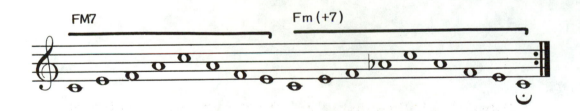

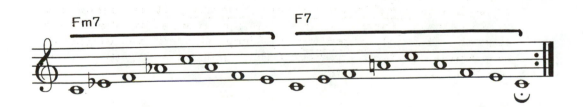

* See pages 21-22 for introductory sets.

CHORD SETS IN THIRD INVERSION

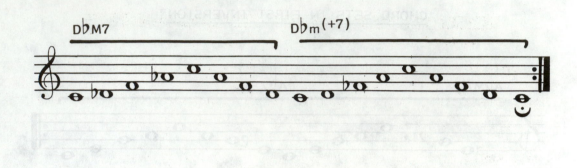

DbM7   Dbm(+7)

*   *   *   *   *

PRIMARY DOMINANT STRUCTURE [V]	CHORD TONE POSSIBILITIES	SUBSTITUTE DOMINANT STRUCTURE [♭II+6]
m13-- M13	E♭-- E	M9-- A9
P11–A11	C--C♯	[N/A]–ROOT*
m9-- M9--A9	A♭-- A--A♯	P5-- A5--M13*
m7	F	M3
d5-- P5--A5	D♭-- D--D♯	ROOT-- m9*–M9*
P4	C	[N/A]
M3	B	m7
ROOT	G	A11

[N/A] = NOT RECOMMENDED

* = ENHARMONIC

The ability to aurally perceive the combined sound of a melodic pitch and its chosen harmonization is an important adjunct to the performer, arranger, and composer. For this reason the above chart in **C major** is presented to help put into focus, at least on paper, the possible combinations of sound which occur when a given pitch is a common chord tone to both **dominant** chords under consideration. The selection of the primary dominant over the substitute dominant, and vice versa, will greatly affect the urgency of the progression and/or the ultimate style of the composition. For the purposes of this abbreviated outline, only vertical alignments of the **dominant** function are presented for study.

It is important to understand that many more variables exist in the process of making the ultimate decision and choice. For instance items such as voice leading, melodic tendencies, color tone considerations, etc., are all intrinsically linked to the eventual selection; however, the harmonic consideration of the thought process begins at this point and for that reason is presented in this manner for study.

Analyze, hear, and play each vertical alignment at the piano from the following examples. Remember that these **dominant** functioning chords are often part of a two chord progression and, as such, represent only half of what could be shown. It would be helpful to the ear to provide an additional chord from the many possibilities already presented in this text.

Finally, it is important to keep the mental process as clear in your mind as possible. Create new possibilities in your mind's eye and ear, and whenever possible, play them at the piano. Check to see if they sound as you imagined them to sound. This is an excellent mode of practice and should be performed as often as possible.

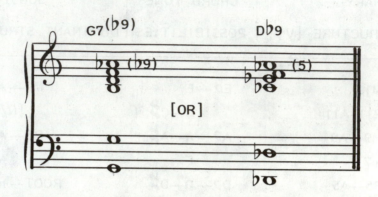

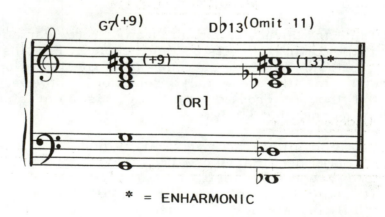

* = ENHARMONIC

The following material concerns the use of scales and how they relate to chords. While most often this material is presented in conjunction with jazz improvisation, it also has relevance for those who are interested in composition. Modes, altered modes, and some esoteric scales are presented along with chord symbols wherever applicable. All have a <u>tonic</u> note of C and should be transposed to all keys for the purposes of daily study.

I–MAJOR TONALITY

The <u>Ionian</u> mode -- or the C Major scale -- and the <u>Lydian</u> mode are related to <u>most</u> chords of the **I–Major Tonality [I–M]** family <u>[**C6, CM7, C6/9,** **CM9(+11), etc.**].</u> See **page 39** of **Part III** for additional information.

I–MINOR TONALITY

The <u>Aeolian</u> mode -- also referred to as the "pure" or "natural" minor scale -- is often utilized with minor chords, particularly in the minor key of the <u>tonic</u> when utilizing the <u>Aeolian</u> scale form [**Cm7, Cm9, etc.**]. However, when the <u>melodic</u> minor scale form is employed, the chordal symbols reflect minor chords with adjusted seventh degrees [**Cm(+7), Cm6, Cm6/9, etc.**]. See **pages 39** & **40** of **Part III** for additional information.

Aeolian Mode

II–MAJOR TONALITY

The <u>Dorian</u> mode is used with most minor chords such as the **II–Major Tonality [II–M]** family [**Cm7, Cm9, Cm11, etc.**]. It would be safe to say that this mode is utilized more than any minor scale form or minor mode form (<u>Phrygian</u> & <u>Aeolian</u>) in jazz. See **pages 39** & **40** of **Part III** for additional information.

II–MINOR TONALITY

The <u>Locrian</u> mode and the Altered Locrian mode are most often used with the **II–Minor Tonality [II–m]** family [**Cm7(–5), etc.**]. See **page 40** of **Part III** for additional information.

Locrian Mode

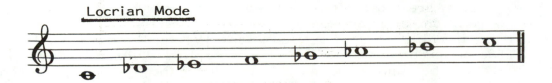

Altered Locrian Mode

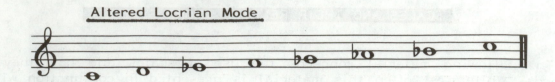

Dominant [V] MAJOR/MINOR

The Mixolydian mode is directly related to the primary dominant chordal structure in major and minor tonalities [C7, C9, C7sus4, C9sus4, etc.]. See pages 40 & 41 of **Part III** for additional information.

Mixolydian Mode

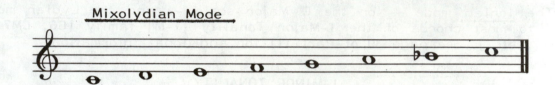

One of the most complex scales related to chords is the doubly-altered Locrian mode. It is often referred to as the "Super Locrian." This mode is composed of two different scales (Whole-tone/Diminished) superimposed upon a Locrian mode. Or, in other words, this scale contains the same tones found in the Altered Lydian mode (lowered seventh degree) placed on the tritone interval above the tonic of the tonality (C to Gb). This scale works best with dominant chords containing lowered or raised ninths and lowered or raised fifths occurring simultaneously [C7(+9,+5), C7(-9,-5), etc.].

Doubly-altered Locrian Mode

THE "BRIDGING" GROUP

The Diminished scale (whole step/half step) is most often played over Fully-Diminished Seventh chord tones. Remember that the Fully-Diminished Seventh chord is entirely symmetrical and, as such, can utilize each chord tone as a tonic scale degree for a minimum of **four** Diminished scales per Fully-Diminished Seventh chord. See **page 40** of **Part III** for additional information.

THE BLUES SCALE

Blues scales are most often utilized as a reservoir of tones for the use of melodic invention and are seldom related directly to chordal structures; however, it is possible to relate a dominant [V] family chord [C7(+9)] in this instance. The interchangeability of the so-called "bluesy" third is not a factor while in the upper octave it provides the necessary raised ninth, enharmonically.

110

Blues Scale

PHRYGIAN MODE

The Phrygian mode is most often found in Flamenco music and other Latin compositions. The use is for the most part melodic in nature and not often related directly to chordal structures.

Phrygian Mode

MINOR PENTATONIC SCALE

Finally, the Pentatonic minor scale is utilized in much the same manner as the blues scale. It acts as a reservoir of tones for melodic invention. Although music theorists, for the most part, are not in complete agreement as to the existence of the Minor Pentatonic scale, most do recognize its potential as a tool in the art of jazz improvisation.

Minor Pentatonic Scale

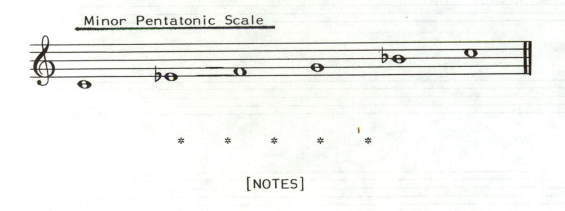

*   *   *   *   *

[NOTES]

Although many harmonic formulas have already been given in **Part IV** of this text, the following series of additional formulas is presented to describe current harmonic devices which exploit the arranger's art of utilizing <u>approach</u> chords. These so-called "approach" devices are usually placed between or before successively strong downbeat chords whose roots are located a whole step apart. Chordal progressions involving I-II-III, IV-V-VI, or III-II-I on successively strong downbeats act as an outline or scheme for the use of any one of three possible harmonic <u>approach</u> devices.

An <u>approach</u> chord is a harmonic device which can function (1) as a fully chromatic alignment of **like-quality** which is aimed from either above or below towards a specific destination, or (2) as a functional <u>dominant</u> directed at a destination chord one-half step away, or (3) as a <u>fully-diminished</u> chordal alignment targeted at a <u>minor seventh</u> chord found one-half step away. The following examples utilize the fully chromatic <u>approach</u> chord as described above in <u>approach</u> device number one. Note carefully the quality of both chords involved at each point of use and the rhythmic flexibility of the concept.

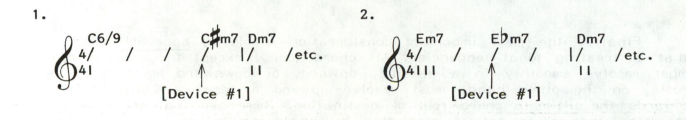

Harmonic devices number 2 and 3 have already been presented in more detail in **Part IV** of this text and will not be duplicated here. However, one comment should be made regarding the use of functional <u>dominants</u> as <u>approach</u> chords. They are best restricted to downward resolutions even though they are occasionally used as lower <u>approach</u> chords. In other words, they are best used as conventional <u>dominant</u> <u>substitutes</u> [♭II+6 or ♭II-Neop.].

The following example provides an attempt at utilizing all three <u>approach</u> devices. Note carefully the added use of internal modification of some of the <u>approach</u> devices and the notion of rhythmic flexibility.

Original

could become:

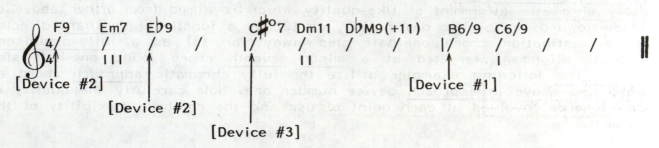

Finally, the most important consideration involving approach chords is that of treating tonal tendencies. All chord tones, except for chordal roots, must resolve smoothly in a passive, upward, or downward manner; chordal roots, on the other hand, must resolve upward or downward by half step towards the ultimate chord root of destination. Remember that it is possible to delay the entire act of resolution by employing internal modification of these approach devices.

*　　*　　*　　*　　*

[8] 1. The **major** key signatures to be identified are the following:

    1. D♭ Major 2. G Major 3. A Major 4. G♭ Major 5. C Major

    6. F♯ Major 7. C♭ Major 8. E Major

[7] 2. The **major** key signatures to be supplied are the following:

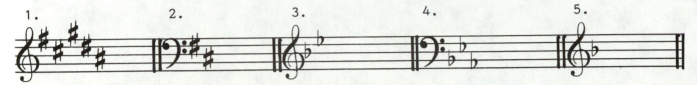

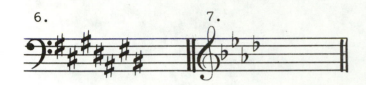

[15] 3. The **harmonic** intervals to be identified are the following:

    1. M3 2. P5 3. M7 4. m2 5. A4 6. m3 7. P4 8. A5 9. m7

    10. M6 11. d4 12. M2 13. m6 14. A2 15. d5

[15] 4. The following completed **harmonic** intervals contain the supplied upper pitches:

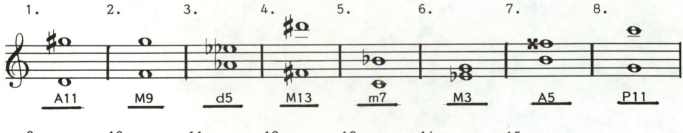

[5] 5. The following completed **harmonic** intervals contain the supplied lower pitches:

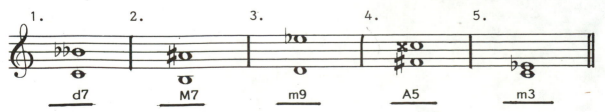

115

INDEX